A refreshingly effective and deeply practical book. Every page offers tools to regain focus and clarity, without the fluff. This is a must-read for anyone looking to cut through the noise and reclaim their space and time.

 – Andrew Pryor, founder & CEO of CIO WaterCooler

A persuasive, inspiring and easy-to-follow resource that you'll return to time and time again. Backed up by science, research and real-life case studies, this book provides an engaging methodology and framework that will motivate you to make meaningful change in your life. Highly recommended.

 – Paul Williamson, group head of talent development,
  ATG Entertainment, and regional chair, Association for
  Coaching

In a world where everything feels urgent and nothing ever feels done, this timely and insightful book offers a powerful antidote to overwhelm. Drawing on over a decade of coaching experience and grounded in a unique three-part model, Ingrid Pope explores clutter not just as a physical nuisance, but as a mental and emotional weight we all carry. With warmth, clarity and deeply human stories, this book guides readers to create space – not just in their homes, but in their lives, minds and hearts.

 – Yvette Forrester, president emeritus of City Women Network

A transformational guide for anyone who feels that they are 'always on'. Ingrid Pope offers practical, deeply relevant tools for decluttering not just your environment, but your mind and emotions too. This book has the power to change how you live across all aspects of your personal, social and working lives. I cannot recommend it highly enough.

 – Tony Scott, CEO of NeuralRays AI

This isn't just about clutter – it's about creating space for contemplation and clarity. With a thoughtful, almost meditative approach, Pope helps you shift your perspective and mindset, turning something as simple as physical, mental and emotional housekeeping into a profoundly important act of self-care. A balm for hectic times.

– Dr Thomas Curran, author of *The Perfection Trap*

As a neurodivergent woman, making changes could often be overwhelming, but the tools and techniques found in this book have held my hand beautifully throughout the process. Written with elegance and insight, it will provide you with just the right level of companionship through all the stages of creating space in your life.

– Jess Mookherjee, author and consultant in public health and wellbeing

At last, a clear and practical guide to uncluttering. Ingrid's approach helped me to simplify so much in my professional life, and with this book, she can help you too.

– Stephen Elsden, former CEO and charity consultant

A much-needed antidote to our increasingly cluttered culture – wise, compassionate and genuinely useful. Read this book if you want to learn how to stop being ruled by what you don't need.

– Lisa Fraser, human-centred design researcher

A transformative read that will help you break free from the overwhelm of physical, mental and emotional clutter. It is an essential guide for anyone seeking to create room for what truly matters and achieve a more balanced and fulfilling existence.

– Michael Randall, associate director infrastructure & operations, global FMCG company

uncluttered.

How to create space
to think, work and live

Ingrid Pope

Uncluttered

ISBN 978-1-917490-00-9

eISBN 978-1-917490-01-6

Published in 2025 by Right Book Press

Printed in the UK in September 2025

Manufactured by

Sue Richardson Associates Ltd.
Studio 6,
9, Marsh Street
Bristol
BS1 4AA

info@therightbookcompany.com

EU Safety Representative

eucomply OÜ
Parnu mnt 139b-14
11317 Tallinn
Estonia

hello@eucompliancepartner.com
+33 756 90241

Contents

Foreword

'What makes a fire burn is space between the logs,
a breathing space...'
– 'Fire', Judy Brown

As someone who has dedicated their life to understanding how
we as human beings develop and grow, I continually aspire to
understand how to enable this process in myself and others.
This dedication has invited me to 'sit with' some key questions,
a central one of which is: 'How do we learn *to get out of our
own way?*' Ingrid expertly deals with what most commonly
limits and *gets in our way* – clutter – and guides the reader with
care, compassion, and non-judgment toward the reality and
opportunity of *decluttering* our lives.

An elegant model of three interrelated dimensions of
decluttering – the physical, mental, and emotional – is defined
and systematically built by Ingrid, resulting in a book that in
its entirety is a comprehensive, valuable and reliable
developmental guide.

I have known Ingrid as a coaching colleague for many years
and I am not surprised by the scope of her understanding and
comprehension of this field of study and her ability to carefully
invite and enable deeper learning. Ingrid offers clear, practical
steps throughout the book that continually guide the reader
in how to embrace and engage fully with the subject in hand
and, most especially, how to learn through their own experience.

Ingrid also brings her own brand of refreshing novelty to the topic – sharing her own ideas and thinking throughout – including the SPACE model, based and built from her extensive experience and practice of working with individuals and groups as an experienced coach, facilitator, and trainer.

Almost everyone I have met and those I continue to meet share challenges associated with cluttering. Feelings of being overwhelmed, for example, by the media, technology and the things we accumulate, commonly resulting in a sense of feeling oppressed, anxious and confined, both at home and at work. This creates a compulsive over-busyness and avid doing. Ingrid thoughtfully illuminates how and why we feel this way and carefully guides the reader in how they can learn to move forward – an opportunity of significant value to everyone.

As well as feeling personally motivated by and wishing to apply the content of this book, I also want to invite a gentle build upon what has been presented and expertly shared. Have you ever wondered what may be the important commodity vital to our growth?

Space.

Human development appears to be intimately associated with a growing sense of inner as well as outer *spaciousness*. This journey of decluttering heralds within us a permitting and emergence of a new 'way of being'. This is the way we become more fully acquainted with, and make conscious, our birthright and namesake, *the human being*. A growing recognition of, and deepening acquaintance with, the person we were, most naturally are, and are destined to become. This learning of how to inhabit our inner spaciousness creates time to truly think, reflect, learn, contemplate, and make meaning of our lives. We can learn how to step back from life's content and clutter to discover the uncluttered space in which we can contemplate the 'more than' for which we may long. Each interrelated level of Ingrid's SPACE model points each of us toward this prospect and possibility. What is revealed is a deeper appreciation of the source of our potential, possibility and purpose, composing what we may consider to be a further spiritual dimension of decluttering vital to our lives.

I support wholeheartedly the value and contribution of Ingrid's work for individuals, groups, organizations, and even wider communities. May we continue to learn together about the essential importance of decluttering and the vital opportunity of *spaciousness*, its role in self-discovery and our own development. And finally, how Ingrid's book and field of work can guide the reader towards their discovery of a deeper sense of purpose, their source of motivation, and reason for being, helping each and all of us to realize the true meaning of our lives, come closer to our real work, and experience a growing sense of fulfillment.

Andrew Machon PhD MA MCC
Author of *A Coaching Secret: How to be an exceptional coach* (2013)

Introduction

In today's world, the pace of life has increased to such an extent that many of us struggle to keep on top of everything. We're bombarded from all directions with demands on our attention, and it takes significant effort and energy to resist distractions and stay focused. Our work and life environments are increasingly complex. Our task lists are never ending; we never get around to doing everything we want to, and often end our days, weeks and months feeling as if time has passed us by and we haven't quite achieved what we intended to. How often do you feel surprised that it's Christmas again?

In this constant rush from one thing to the next, there's no time to think, to reflect on our experiences, to contemplate our longer-term goals or delve into our deeper selves to consider what we truly long for, what fulfills us. My experience of these very feelings led me to view the world through the lens of the clutter that we're confronted with all the time, not only the clutter that's thrown at us from all sides, but also the clutter that we've accumulated over the years that now gets in the way of our effectiveness, our life, ourselves.

In my work studying clutter and its effects on people, I have identified three different forms – the physical clutter of the spaces in which we live and work; the mental clutter that overfills our heads; and the emotional clutter that drives our actions, often unconsciously. Each form will have a different impact on you, but they're all interconnected, and together they contribute to making you feel stressed and overwhelmed. Based on these findings, I have created a three-part model, each part addressing a different form of clutter.

Now, one thing that I repeat all the time is that clutter in itself isn't necessarily a bad thing. I'm not advocating that everything needs to go, that pure minimalism is the only way forward for a better life. What I'm saying is that all of us need to pay attention to the clutter in our world and notice when it becomes excessive and gets in our way. That's when it's time to do something about it. And doing something about it means paying close attention to what's there and being active in choosing it to be there. I call it being choiceful in what we surround ourselves with and carry with us, rather than letting stuff, thoughts and emotions simply be there by default.

When I left my senior IT role in the corporate world after 16 years, I knew that I wanted to work in this area of decluttering and creating space and knew that there was far more to it than only the physical space. Physical space is often tied in with mental clutter, and even more entangled with emotional clutter.

I became credentialed as a professional certified coach with the International Coaching Federation and have been helping clients create space for more than ten years now. Alongside one-to-one coaching, I also run group programs for individuals, workshops for businesses, and speak at business conferences about decluttering for effectiveness. I feel strongly that unless you look closely at where your focus and attention are going, you will continue to feel as if life is passing you by, and I'm hopeful that this book will make you see why that matters.

Cathy joined my decluttering program because she wanted to clear some of the excessive physical clutter in her home, which had been plaguing her for a few years. She had a bit too much stuff to fit into her storage areas, and for reasons she wasn't clear about herself, was not getting started with tidying it up. A successful job and many other ambitions were keeping her busy and she kept putting off this task, year after year. By joining my group, she wanted to set aside the time to get this done, find the motivation to finally address it, and learn a few new techniques around decluttering plus some insights into what was holding her back. What originally seemed like a matter of headspace and attention revealed something else.

As she progressed through the program, Cathy found that the challenge wasn't with her physical clutter. I have often seen this – the physical mess is generally the symptom, and the work is in understanding what lies beneath it. In this case, the process brought to light some stories Cathy was telling herself about how she should be in the world and the incredibly high expectations she had of herself, of which she was inevitably falling short. Even more impactfully, she uncovered some emotional clutter around old family patterns that affected her more than she had realized. All this mental and emotional clutter was her stumbling block and this is what needed to be addressed.

In the whirlwind of her day-to-day life, Cathy had successfully blocked out all these buried feelings and though they crept out every now and again in unexpected ways, especially when she was stressed or tired, she had developed efficient coping strategies to keep her emotions under wraps. Her busyness had become her avoidance mechanism, though it came with a few unhappy side effects such as feeling slightly lost and an overall sense of drifting. The stress of her job combined with the complexities of the world and modern living had taken up so much of Cathy's headspace and waking hours that she had no capacity to address her deeper longings. Embarking on a decluttering journey through the portal of wanting to tidy her home opened many unexpected and surprising doors for her.

Maybe you also feel overwhelmed, living in this world of too much and too fast. You feel out of control, no longer choiceful of where you put your time, energy and attention. You have lost sight of the bigger picture and the purpose of what you are doing. And because you feel overwhelmed by all this clutter, you don't know where to start in your effort to create space, to regain a sense of balance and control over your life. Does this sound familiar?

This book is based on a learning program that I created around my three-part model. It is the product of my research as well as my experience from taking groups of participants through the course, and hundreds of hours of working with professionals and leaders individually across many different sectors and industries. In it, I bring together both material from various scientific fields as well as real-life examples to give a rounded picture of the different topics covered. I offer many tools and ideas, some of which you might find useful now, and others less so. Simply take from it what you need at this time.

Clutter will affect everyone differently. Neurodiversity is much talked about nowadays, and clutter is a topic that comes up in many conversations I have in this space, in particular in relation to ADHD and finding headspace. We all have our own unique brains, our own ways of thinking, our own lived experience, and we all have different areas that we find challenging.

What I have learned from working with all my clients is that there are common threads, and these are the learnings that I share within this book. I bring structure to what feels intangible and unwieldy, and offer a simple set of steps to begin tackling what can seem completely indomitable. Often, my clients don't know *how* to go about creating more space for themselves, so that's where I come in and why I have written this book.

My aim is to help you shift some of the clutter that you no longer need and create space for whatever it is you wish for instead. Because all the while you are at – or even beyond – your capacity, there is no room for anything new, anything more, anything different. This book will be the catalyst for change in your life and work.

The concept of decluttering might seem to relate mainly to the domestic sphere, and much has already been written about that, but other areas of your life can also become affected by too much clutter. Decluttering is about much more than organizing your home. Whether you want better quality thinking at work, more space for creativity in your projects, improved health or deeper relationships with those who matter the most to you, this book will guide the way.

More about the three different forms of clutter

The way that I approach a mountain of too much of everything is by breaking it down into the following three areas.

Physical clutter

When you think of the word 'clutter', what immediately comes to mind is probably physical clutter. It is the stuff that you can see, that is covering various surfaces in your home or office, piled into the corners or behind cupboard doors, filling up spare rooms and generally getting in your way.

Whether it is a messy workspace that distracts you from deep concentration, an untidy kitchen that interferes with healthy eating, an overflowing wardrobe containing nothing to wear that makes you feel good about yourself, or endless repeated arguments about whose stuff is lying around, physical clutter is likely to touch every aspect of your life. The first part is all about this physical clutter, why it matters and the impact it has on you, your work and your relationships with those around you.

Mental clutter

The second part looks at your mental clutter. You tend to notice this type of clutter less because it is intangible. You can't see it, hold it, put it in a drawer, but it can get in your way and trip you up just as easily as your physical stuff.

Learning and growth come from self-reflection, but if your head is constantly full of thoughts and distractions, chances are you never get around to this type of contemplation. How often do you catch yourself attempting to multitask during a meeting? When do you make the time for creativity and new thinking to move your projects forward?

Businesses are spending big money to steal your attention in ever cleverer ways, so protecting your brain and ability to focus are critical. Your mind and your thinking are your most valuable assets, so learning to shed what is unnecessary and being mindful of what you let in will transform your effectiveness.

Emotional clutter

The third part focuses on emotional clutter. Emotions are a fundamental part of who you are and how you live your life. They drive your behavior at every turn, and you often don't even realize it or notice them. They affect not only what you do, but also how you do things and how you interact with others. It is also the part that might be the scariest to look at and that you might want to bypass at first, and that's OK.

When you're ready, turning your attention to your emotional clutter, how it affects you and when it gets in your way will give you vital information when it comes to making changes in your life. Whether you want to adopt a new behavior, take a different career path, or make any number of other big or small life changes, understanding your emotional landscape will make the transition that much smoother.

The three types of clutter that form my model are often interrelated. Stuff rarely sits neatly in one single category, but the likelihood is that you will notice or be aware of one type of clutter more than another or have a sense that one category is more prevalent in your life than another. If that's the case, that might be the place to begin. Paying attention to what type of clutter you're dealing with will be the starting point of any decluttering journey.

1

Creating space in your life

5-step de-cluttering method

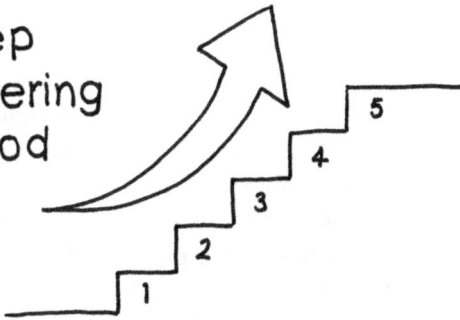

This book is organized into three parts, each covering one of the types of clutter. You can either read through all three parts in the order presented or dip into whichever area feels the most relevant to you at this moment.

In each part, I will explain how that type of clutter might affect you, give pointers as to what to pay attention to, and then run through my five-step method to reduce the clutter and create more space in that area. I will describe the decluttering method in detail in this chapter as it applies to every type of clutter, then I will revisit it at the end of each of the three parts to make it specific and concrete. But before you start doing anything, I want to take a moment to examine what the purpose might be for you in embarking on this decluttering project.

Tapping into your purpose

All the while you don't know why you are doing what you are doing and being who you are being, you don't fully have agency around your behavior. You operate on autopilot and follow the patterns and habits you have developed over your lifetime. So, if you want a change, such as starting to tackle clutter of whatever type, and find this is something you are struggling to do, then a useful starting point is to identify what your purpose is for doing it in the first place. Because the one thing that affects everything that you do, how you do it, who you are and how the world sees you is your purpose. Tapping into the purpose of your resolve to declutter is an essential part of helping to motivate you and keep you going when the change becomes hard. And there might be some hard work involved along the way!

Take some time to think about what your purpose is for engaging in a decluttering process right now. Sometimes the real purpose isn't immediately visible and is hidden under a few layers of intangible clutter. It might be worth asking yourself the 'why?' question a few times to uncover your deeper motivation.

Example: I want to declutter my office so that I can work more effectively.

Why? So that I can reduce the distractions and feel more professional at work.

Why? So that I can spend more time on strategic topics rather than dealing with my inbox all the time, making my work more fulfilling.

Why? So that I can feel better about myself and be happier.

Why? So that I can be a better role model of self-worth for my children.

Getting to the true reason behind why you do what you do will become your driver, and the more meaningful your purpose is to you, the deeper you will feel the desire to follow it.

Setting a goal

If your purpose is all about *why* you are doing something, your goal will be *what* you are setting out to do. The area of goal setting is interesting. In a broader sense, having goals in our lives is fundamental to our wellbeing. Maybe, like many people, you have experienced periods of time (whether it be a few hours, days, or more) when you felt aimless. Sometimes, this was a welcome change after a particularly busy time. At other moments, though, it can result in a feeling of lethargy, boredom, a sense of being disconnected from the rest of the world, or several other feelings, too.

These goals can be anything you want them to be. They don't have to be life-altering/planet-changing/far-reaching events (though they might be!). They can be small things, maybe that only you will ever see and experience, but which will give you a sense of satisfaction and make you feel good about yourself.

One of the things to take notice of here is your emotional clutter, and the reason for this is that emotions are important in determining action. At a basic level, they inform you of a threat that might require you to run for your life. On a more complex level, they have a role to play in your motivation. So, if you think about goals that you might have, understanding the emotional clutter that might get in the way of your motivation to achieve those goals will be hugely helpful to your success.

Emotions are a powerful force. They are the response to a situation, the product of large amounts of information gathered from all senses and then filtered and processed through various parts of the brain. It is fascinating to look at these forces at play in terms of reaching goals. Emotions often get triggered to keep you safe, so understanding how they can hold you back from trying out new things is important. They sometimes want to keep you in what is known and therefore comfortable. However, they can also help you move toward your desired endpoint through the power of rewards. Our brains are clever like that! I'll look at this in more detail in Chapter 11 when I examine emotional regulation.

But first, coming back to your decluttering work, what is your goal right now? I would encourage you to be as specific as you can. The more tangible you are able to make your goal, the more real it will feel. You might ask yourself questions like these:

- What will be different for me once I've achieved this goal?
- What will it look like once I'm there?
- What will it feel like?
- Is this goal something that I want, or is it something that others want for me? (Your motivation will be stronger if the desire for change comes from you.)
- How comfortable am I with my goal? Is it aligned with my values or is there an incongruence at some level? If so, how can I adjust this goal to match my personal values? Or do my values need updating, decluttering and adjusting?
- What emotions am I noticing in myself when I articulate my goal(s)?
- Who can help me stick to my commitments?

Writing down your goals and discussing them with others makes you more likely to persevere with them and see them through.

Once you have gained some clarity around why you want to declutter and what your future uncluttered space might look and feel like, here is how you will go about doing this work.

The SPACE method

One of the things that drew me to coaching as a profession is the focus that is put on effecting change. Clients come to me because they want to gain deeper knowledge about themselves, but also to couple new insights with a move to action. It is the shift from solely thinking about a situation to doing something about it that I find so attractive, as it is the energy released by taking action that allows my clients to see how they can do things differently and shape their trajectory any which way they want.

1. Survey

The first step of any process is to survey the current state of the landscape. The reality of your clutter can feel overwhelming, and the single biggest challenge my clients usually have is not knowing where to start. The first step is always to break it down into pieces that you can tackle one after the other.

This is achieved by looking at and truly seeing what you are dealing with. This takes time and might require several visits. You want to take in everything that is there that you want to sort through. You want to start identifying all the different types of things in the landscape so that you can get your head around what might need to shift.

Now this might sound easy, but it can be a difficult task to carry out. Sometimes the reality of the stacks, boxes, wardrobes, garage, thoughts, feelings is too much to face. But if you are serious about engaging with the process, you need to know what is there. You are simply gathering data about the reality, removing any associated feelings, thoughts or other self-critical inner chatter, as none of this judgment is helpful.

A change in perspective can give you a fresh view. The further away you are from a situation, the more clearly you can see the bigger picture. So, to survey your landscape properly, to really see what is there, you need to stand and look from a vantage point that is slightly distanced. For your physical clutter, this means you might stand in the corner of a room, in a doorway, or you can look at things in your mind's eye from somewhere completely different and removed. You want to take a few steps away from the actual items so that you can see them as a collective rather than individual pieces.

For your mental clutter as well as your emotional clutter, putting a bit of distance between yourself and the thoughts and feelings will allow you to see them more clearly too. When you are caught up in a negative repetitive rumination or the drama of a situation, that is unlikely to be a good place for level-headed reflection. Taking a step back and observing your thoughts and feelings from a slightly removed place – both in terms of location and time – will give you many insights that are not visible when you are in the actual situation.

Positive psychology (visited in Chapter 2 and Chapter 10) is also useful at this point. If you approach the survey step under the influence of positivity – you might feel good about your resolve to start the process, or you might hold onto a vision of the new space created, or look forward to a reward you might treat yourself to for the hard work you are undertaking – you literally see more and take in the bigger picture more easily.

2. Plan

The second step of the process is to look at all the different areas and types of things, thoughts and feelings that you have observed in your landscape, and to apply a choice as to whether you are happy with the situation or whether something needs to change. Once you have that view of what you want to choicefully keep or shift, you can start forming a plan for how to go about doing this. I will help you break everything down into different tasks that you can then prioritize in the order in which you want to get them done.

This prioritization process is deeply personal and completely up to you. My challenge to you is to simply be truthful with yourself and make choices that feel right and perhaps stretch you, rather than choices that might feed an avoidance habit. Knowing yourself, how you operate and what motivates you are all useful pieces of information in this process. Equally valuable are the purpose of why you want to declutter in the first place and the goals you identified earlier, as these can help inform the order in which you address the different tasks.

Once you have a sense of the sequence in which you will work on the different spaces and areas in your landscape, you can set out a plan of what you will do and when you will do it by. I suggest capturing tasks that are small and achievable in a single sitting so that you can see the progress you are making and feel the satisfaction of ticking them off from your list. This will give you a great sense of pride and achievement!

To produce this plan, it can be useful to ask yourself *when* you might be most effective for doing this type of work. Interesting research into the 'time of day effect' highlights how our energy levels differ during the day, and what activities are best done when (Pink 2018). For example, I find mornings are a good time for concentrated and focused mental work, whereas I perform creative tasks far better in the afternoons or evenings. Tap into your energy levels and determine when you would be the most productive at tackling different projects.

3. Act

After identifying what you want to shift from your current landscape and having put together a plan of how and when to do this, it's time to execute your plan. This step can seem daunting because of the scale of the work and because you might have attempted it in the past and not had the success you had hoped for. But as with everything, persevering and taking it one step at a time will get you through.

You will have your own preferences for how you like to work, what motivates you, when is a good time for you to do things, and how to keep yourself going. Some people like to block time in their calendars to perform certain tasks. For others, this is too constraining and they prefer to give themselves a time frame within which to get something done. Others like to team up with someone, either as an accountability buddy or to do the work together. We are all different, so experiment with different approaches and do what works well for you. My invitation here is to connect with how you work at your best and to believe in your abilities and skills to get this done.

4. Celebrate

Have you ever noticed how, when you ask someone how a particular project is going, they'll usually say 'It's progressing, but there's still a lot to do', or some variation on that theme? We are wired to completely disregard what we have done and focus instead on what is still left to do. That is why the fourth step of the decluttering method is to celebrate.

I'm big on celebrating. I don't mean that I crack out the champagne every five minutes, however tempting that might be, but I do notice what achievements others are minimizing and ignoring, and I pause to acknowledge them. I feel it is so important to recognize and celebrate every success, however small.

As with everything we set out to achieve, it can become difficult to stick with a project for the long haul. This is especially true for the bigger tasks, or some activities that we find difficult. We easily revert to our familiar and comfortable patterns. So, what is your typical strategy? How do you keep going? And, equally important, what do you already know now that is likely to trip you up down the line? What is typical for you and what would you like to do differently this time?

Going back to your plan from Step 3 and the list of activities you identified, each one that is completed can be a reason for celebration. This can take any form you like and that works for you: putting your feet up for an hour, going for a run, enjoying a walk on your own, calling a friend, taking the time to listen to a podcast, treating yourself to a massage, giving yourself space for a bath, taking a good book to bed… Only you will know what is a powerful motivator for you and will keep your momentum going.

It is easy to diminish your achievements and gloss over them. In some cultures, it is frowned upon to display pride in yourself, to pat yourself on the back for a job well done. So, it is easier to be modest and consider it as 'nothing'. But you also need to see progress in your endeavors. You need to see that you are moving forward in order to maintain the drive to carry on. It is important to pause and celebrate these steps forward, even if you do so only internally and to yourself.

5. Evaluate

The fifth and final step of the decluttering method is the evaluation. Decluttering and creating physical, mental and emotional space will involve many iterations of the process, one for each of the areas you have identified in your survey and have mapped out in your plan. You will go through this cycle numerous times.

As with every process that is repetitive, taking the time at the end of each iteration to reflect on what has worked well and what you might do differently next time to make it better is an invaluable exercise for self-growth and success. Making some notes on this to review at a later date will also be useful as some time may have elapsed between your experience and when you go into the next cycle.

The key here is to understand that you are gathering data. You merely want to notice and record your experience, without judgment of any sort. Your inner judge, the one that constantly judges you, others and your circumstances, is your strongest and most powerful saboteur (Chamine 2012). Judgment does not help you here – or anywhere else for that matter – but instead causes mental chatter as well as emotional clutter, and it gets in the way of achieving what you set out for yourself. Noticing when your judge saboteur kicks in and clutters your view is useful. Simply capturing the truth about how things went is what will be invaluable for your continued progress.

Dismantling a few barriers

When it comes to decluttering, the task might seem so big that it can feel like a huge hurdle to climb over to get started. And we know that when things get tough, we all have a natural and strong tendency to stay put. All change is scary, and our brains will do everything they can to keep us safe by keeping us right where we are, right in the familiar – more on that later.

The usual difficulties that my clients bring up to explain why they struggle to make a start or keep going with the process are as follows:

'I don't have enough time for this right now!'
Well, here is the thing: there is enough time. All you need is a minute or two to pick up one thing, notice one thought or one emotion, decide whether to keep it or not, and then put it where you have decided it should go. Of course, ideally you would repeat this process for a number of items, thoughts or emotions, not just the one, at any one time. And perhaps you need to think about reconfiguring a room or a storage area or consider how you could experiment with a new behavior that will need to be identified. But this doesn't have to be done all at once. Make a start by picking up one thing.

'I'm a messy person; that's simply who I am.'
I hear this all the time but let me challenge that statement. You might think that you are a messy person, or indeed that you are a messy person right now, but that is not a reason for you to be one in the future. You can decide what type of person you want to be starting right now. You could, for example, be someone who is learning a new skill about how to be tidy, or you could be someone who enjoys a tidy space and creates that for themselves, or you could be someone who has decided that they wanted a new start and tidying their environment is the first step toward this future. You decide exactly what type of person you want to be, and your past behaviors do not determine who you must be in the future.

'I don't have the willpower to stick with it.'
When we put our minds to something, we are unstoppable. Whether it be a hobby, a project that we are passionate about, or a friend who needs some help, we find all the time and energy in the world to get done what needs to be done. This is because we care about the outcome, we have an emotional attachment to

it, and usually we know why we are doing it in the first place. It's the same story with a decluttering process. Once you tap into your purpose, into why you are doing this right now, into why it matters to you, and more importantly into what the costs are to you of not doing it, you will find the willpower to stick with it and carry on.

'I'll do it tomorrow/next week/when…'
This is a common one. It is certainly familiar to me, and it is a great way to put something off for what you want to believe is a short time but ends up being forever. You may use this excuse to make yourself feel safe and in control, to feel as if you have a plan, and that is just what you need right now. But plans are only any good if they are acted upon and carried through at some point. So, how about trying a new line: 'I will do this right now and see how it goes.'

'I'm frightened of what I'll find/uncover/will happen when I let my guard down and start looking.'
Whether you are thinking about looking at your physical clutter or considering your mental or emotional clutter, anything that will disturb the current situation will likely feel uncomfortable. You are considering addressing things, thoughts, feelings, that are currently stowed away and hidden out of sight. And this can be scary. I can't promise you that there is a magic wand that will make it easy. But what I can say is this: the fear of what *might* happen is usually far worse than what does happen. And sometimes, it also turns out to be not nearly as hard as you thought.

Yes, I am sure that you will have many good reasons as to why things are the way they are for you now. As I mentioned earlier, clutter can easily feel overwhelming. The expression 'not seeing the wood for the trees' comes to mind. We stay stuck in our familiar landscape, and it can feel almost insurmountable to do anything about it.

Each part of this book contains plenty of ideas of things you could try, some of which you will find useful immediately, and others that will perhaps be less relevant to you at this moment. My encouragement to you is to take what you need right now and be bold in experimenting with the methods I've suggested. Play around with them, test things out and see what starts creating more spaciousness in your life. It will be worth it.

Chapter summary

▶ Spend some time defining your purpose for decluttering right now, as it will act as a strong guide for why you want to do this work.

▶ Determining your goal(s) for what you want to achieve will drive your actions.

▶ The five-step decluttering method (SPACE) will be applied to all types of clutter as a step-by-step guide to getting this done:
  1. Survey
  2. Plan
  3. Act
  4. Celebrate
  5. Evaluate

▶ You are likely to be telling yourself many stories about why decluttering will be difficult. And that is just what they are: stories, not facts.

Part 1

Creating physical space

2

Clutter is about
more than just mess

When I was 15 years old, I was sitting on my bed one evening doing my homework when I looked up and took in my room. It was a messy room. There were all manner of things lying around on the floor and the few surfaces that I had. This was the usual state of my bedroom.

For some reason, on that evening, a thought popped into my head: 'I don't like this mess very much.' I hadn't paid much attention to it before, but on that day, it bothered me. Maybe I had been sitting cross-legged on my bed for too long, felt stiff and was annoyed that I couldn't sit at my desk. On that day, something clicked about the way my surroundings felt. I continued to look around my room and noticed two things:

1. There was a lot of stuff (mainly school related, such as paperwork and books).
2. There was nowhere to put all this stuff.

In looking around my room, in realizing what needed to be stored away, I was surveying it from the vantage point of my bed – the first step in the SPACE method.

I realized what I needed. I spoke to my dad and asked for a bigger desk as well as shelves on the wall (the Plan step). Eventually, these things materialized (through Action) and my room was immediately transformed. I had space to put things where they belonged, a desk that was big enough to hold the various materials I needed for homework and even my new sewing machine, and my floor was clear. I felt better, was able to concentrate better, and was more productive all round. Well, as much as any slightly grumpy teenager might be at least. Ever since, I have had a sense of how much my physical environment mattered to how I feel, how I work, how I live, my peace of mind.

One of my early clients, a successful senior leader managing complex projects and many staff, once said to me: 'There's nowhere I can talk about this stuff.' By 'stuff', she meant the various feelings of self-criticism, frustration, shame and all-round helplessness that she felt about having a messy home and not liking it.

What you surround yourself with matters. How you feel in the rooms of your own home matters on so many levels. When everything doesn't look just so, and your 'just so' will be different from the next person's, do you, like this client of mine, see it as a personal failure?

This early client was highly capable in her work and respected in her field. That she couldn't keep her house organized was something she kept separate from her work persona, and she couldn't reconcile why she couldn't deal with what seemed like a simple activity at home, when she successfully completed far more complex tasks at work.

Since then, I have had so many similar conversations. I notice how many people are affected by the mess in their homes, and more importantly what the consequences are in the various areas of their lives. This clutter has an impact on their relationships with those around them, on the amount of headspace that is taken up by thinking about it, their concentration levels at work, how they socialize, or not – by feeling too ashamed to invite anyone into their home – and most importantly how they feel about themselves. Mess reaches far beyond what you can see.

Wanting to own things is nothing new

'Don't own so much clutter that you will be relieved to
see your house catch fire.'
– Wendell Berry, *Farming: A hand book* (2011)

Tangible messiness is what we immediately think of when we hear the word clutter, and everyone has a story about it. When I meet people and share what I do, they always tell me a story about their garage, their attic or their spare room. In our world of consumerism, many of us have too much stuff. I once spoke at an event for a financial institution where two unrelated members of the audience told me an identical story about their bicycles, which could only be reached by climbing over boxes in their garage! We go through our lives accumulating things from a variety of different sources – purchases we make, souvenirs we buy, gifts we receive, heirlooms we inherit – and these things can slowly but surely take over our space.

The desire to surround ourselves with nice things is not a new one. Back in the Victorian era, when the Industrial Revolution brought down manufacturing costs and made things more affordable, it was a sign of wealth to have as many decorative items on display as possible. Rooms were often overstuffed with ornaments and pictures hanging on walls, sometimes up to two or three layers deep. Imagine that! Thinking of that decor today conjures up rather oppressive feelings.

The Arts and Crafts movement arrived in the 1860s as a response to this excess and favored far more stripped-back spaces. William Morris, known today for his activism in that movement and his textile designs, famously penned the statement: 'Have nothing in your houses that you do not know to be useful, or believe to be beautiful.' (1882)

In more recent years, Marie Kondo took the world by storm with her concepts and ideas around decluttering, encouraging us to pick up every single item we own and to only keep those that spark joy. Her continued success shows how much this topic speaks to people, and that decluttering can sometimes be a challenging process because of the complex relationships we have developed with our stuff.

The pursuit of ownership is one of the most powerful forces driving our behavior from a very early age and all through our lives (Hood 2020). With such a strong desire and need to possess things, it comes as no surprise that tackling an excessive accumulation of belongings requires real energy and drive.

Clutter is a risky business

Clutter kills. OK, that might sound a bit extreme, but when taken to excess, that can indeed be the end result. It's easy to imagine all manner of accidents happening in spaces that are cluttered, from tripping over items on the floor to being struck by piles of stuff falling over. In Chapter 3, I will talk more about how clutter is linked to stress levels and what the implications of sustained raised levels of stress can be. Here, however, is a story of a slightly different nature.

It's Friday 24 September 2010. Around 5 pm, a cigarette butt is thrown out of the window of an apartment in the 30-floor block at 200 Wellesley Street East in Toronto, Canada, and lands on combustible material stored on the balcony of apartment 2424. It starts a fire.

The fire services are called, and they expect a routine fire. But what they find is a six-alarm fire, the highest level Toronto Fire Services assign to a blaze. And the reason for this unexpected intensity of fire is that apartment 2424 is occupied by a compulsive hoarder. The accumulation and therefore density of paper as well as flammable plastics and synthetics causes a disproportionately high fuel load in a small space, resulting in a much earlier flashover point than expected. 'I'd never witnessed an apartment fire that required firefighting operations over a prolonged period of eight hours,' said fire chief William Stewart (2010).

The flashover point is when a fire has built up so much heat in a confined space that everything within it auto-ignites and combusts simultaneously. About 30 years ago, this point was reached just under 30 minutes into a fire. Nowadays, with items made from many more synthetic materials and plastics, this flashover point can be reached within three to four minutes. Fires now reach levels of intensity that were unimaginable a few years ago, and as a result they can create their own weather events and take on completely new patterns of behavior, leaving firefighters struggling to get them under control (Vaillant 2023).

Fire services are now well aware of the risks of dealing with properties occupied by compulsive hoarders and are trained to be on the lookout for homes at risk. Social services are also involved, doing their best to help those with a hoarding disorder, the aim being not to throw everything away, but to work compassionately in making their homes a bit safer.

Even if we are not suffering from a hoarding disorder, our clutter levels matter. People often say to me: 'But isn't clutter the sign of a creative mind?' or 'It's an organized mess; I know exactly where everything is and this works for me.' And some people might well work better in a cluttered space.

The key is simply to be honest with yourself. Does your clutter enable your efficiency, or does it hinder you in some way? What is the risk involved in keeping the clutter? And going back to the analogy of the fire, how far away is your flashover point, both in terms of stuff but also figuratively in terms of energy and workload? Has the stuff taken on a life of its own and is it no longer under your control? These can be uncomfortable questions, but if you only stay in what's comfortable, nothing will ever change. Then again, how do you know when too much is too much?

The 'time to tidy' measure

When we talk about clutter, we often use words that describe something uncountable, something collective, like stuff, mess, disorganization. And when we use these terms, it is difficult to be specific about them: how messy is messy? How much stuff is too much stuff?

To introduce a way of quantifying this stuff, I created a metric that I have found useful in my discussions around clutter and room tidiness. I have called it 'time to tidy'. You want to live in a space that is inviting and works for you, and this is unlikely to be a permanent show home. A certain level of messiness is simply a sign of life in your home. It certainly is in mine!

The 'time to tidy' measure is the time that it takes to tidy a specific room or area to a satisfactory standard, or visitor standard, that you are comfortable with. Different rooms will have a different ideal 'time to tidy' depending on their use. For example, I am relaxed about living with a 'one hour to tidy' dining room. It is a space that I only use for eating when I have guests, and the rest of the time it is used for whatever I happen to need it for. If I can get it guest tidy within an hour, I feel I am in control of the situation. Much longer and it starts to feel unsettling and slightly stressful. For the spare bedroom, my aim is 'two hours to tidy'. For the kitchen, it is '30 minutes to tidy'.

It is easy to underestimate the side effects that messiness and clutter can have on you. Alongside the resulting increased stress levels, there are other impacts. For example, if my dining room is in a state that means it requires a big effort before it can host anyone, I will probably not be inclined to invite friends over for a meal, even if I love entertaining and it is an important part of my life. I will feel as if the effort is too big, I don't have the time to clear up as well as prepare food, and my social life slowly shrinks.

Similarly, if the guest bedroom is far from being usable for anyone to sleep in, I will hesitate before inviting someone to stay, even if I love having visitors. Your clutter can literally shrink your world through the space that it takes up. Not only that, but your clutter can also shrink your mental and emotional worlds by making you miss out on the experiences it denies you.

Of course, we will all have varying views on how tidy a room needs to be to welcome guests – and it might even depend on the guest! – or how tidy a home office needs to be when we are receiving a client. But I find this metric helpful as it allows me to put some words around a concept (messiness) that can feel difficult to measure. It also gives me a language with which to have a conversation about clutter in a factual and unemotional manner.

If you were to reflect on the spaces in which you live and work, what are the 'times to tidy' that you would feel happy or comfortable with? How far from these 'times to tidy' are you at the moment? These observations can help inform your plans when you follow the decluttering method to create physical space.

Clutter and positive psychology

After looking at clutter from the perspective of volume, considering how *much* stuff you might have in your space and whether you are happy with the quantity of things around you, I want to shift the focus now on *what* makes up your clutter.

Most people have a treasured old teddy bear or several favorite books. You may have other items that flood you with a warm and happy feeling when you pick them up or look at them. If your house were on fire, these are the items you would save!

I happened to be moving house when I came across positive psychology for the first time. I was instantly fascinated by the effects that positivity could have. You can probably imagine that feeling positive about one thing might have an impact on how you feel about another thing, and that this will probably also impact how you feel about life as a whole and be good for your mental health in general.

What was new to me and got me thinking was the physiological effect that positivity could have on us, too. In an experiment with children, those given a small gift before taking a test scored higher than those who had not received anything. A different study, by tracking eye movement, showed that people who were under the influence of positivity looked more broadly at pictures and took more in. Positivity changed their physiology and allowed them to see more of the world (Fredrickson 2009).

If positivity has such an impact on us and makes us happier, more effective and literally allows us to see a bigger picture more clearly, then the stuff that we choose to surround ourselves with, to carry with us and to keep in our space, is hugely important. Whether our items make us feel positive or negative can have a real bearing on our lives.

Now, let me come back to my house move a few years back. I was moving in with my husband-to-be after both of us had been on our own for some time. We each had a full household and all this stuff now needed to fit into a single home. Of course, decisions needed to be made about what to keep and what to let go of, and some of these decisions would be easier to make than others.

With positivity newly at the forefront of my mind, I realized that there were many things that I did not need to hold on to. I found pieces of clothing that made me feel unhappy because they didn't fit anymore, or because I had never worn them. I had books that made me feel bad because they were classics that I should have read, but they just never tempted me.

It was time to look at my stuff through the lens of positivity. I decided not to keep anything that made me feel negative in any way, even though some things were easier to discard or pass on than others. Going through the process of moving house, of handling every single thing that I owned, allowed me to make an active choice about what I was deciding to keep.

Around that time, I also came across Marie Kondo and her way of viewing clutter from the perspective of sparking joy (Kondo 2014). The concept is similar: it is about tapping into how our things make us feel. Having things isn't a problem in itself; it is either having too many things or having the wrong things that can start having a negative impact on us and our lives.

Your home is your shelter from the world; it is where you rest and regenerate. How you feel in this shelter is hugely important because it affects every single other aspect of your life too. When you look around as you go through your home, how do you feel about the items you see? Do different spaces bring up different feelings?

For a while, I was in a job that involved me spending a few nights a week away, and for budget reasons those nights were spent in lower-end lodgings. I found that simply knowing I was going to spend the night somewhere I didn't want to be affected how I felt at work, even though I, the office and my colleagues were all unchanged.

How you feel about your home matters. How you feel about your workplace matters. The physical environment you are in makes a big difference to how you feel, how effective you are, how well you think and how good a job you do.

Putting aside your inner chatter

I'll be talking more about mental clutter in Part 2, but I want to touch on it here as our different types of clutter are often interlinked!

'I really should do something about this mess.'

'I can't believe I've let it get this bad. I'm hopeless.'

'I'm such a messy person. I've always been told that, and here's the proof.'

'I'm useless, and I'm ashamed by the state of this space.'

I hear these lines, or a variation on them, all the time. We so often have a self-critical inner voice that is judging us in some way for having let the space get messy, for not being tidy, for not knowing how to tidy or organize a space, for what others will think…

This inner chatter, this judgmental and critical voice, will sound familiar. It has been holding the same talk, probably for years, and repeatedly highlights your faults and shortcomings in the tidiness department. Perhaps it looks out for your faults in other departments too.

This inner chatter can come from any number of places: from previous actual or perceived criticism by others, from a sense of inadequacy, from a dissatisfaction, from a feeling of not being good enough. Wherever this self-talk comes from, its aim is to keep you in your place and stop you from doing something brave or different. But also, wherever this self-talk comes from, you can change it. And the easiest way of doing that is to produce a new narrative that you can tell yourself instead.

One of my favorite words is 'yet'. Instead of saying 'I'm a messy person who's no good at tidying,' you might say, 'I haven't found a way to organize my stuff that works for me *yet*.' This can be a difficult thing to do. I'm talking about breaking the pattern of a familiar inner chatter and belief system that you either developed for yourself, or more likely, someone else put into your head at some point. It has been with you for a long time and even if it doesn't make you feel particularly good about yourself, it is what you know and feels like the truth. Breaking out of that well-known cycle will feel unfamiliar, novel, probably even scary.

Many people undertake a big decluttering process when they are going through some life change: they might be changing their career, beginning a new relationship, shifting to a different lifestyle. In that case, the bigger transformation is perhaps easier to see, and the letting go of the old is something that is happening alongside something else. When you start a decluttering process on its own, with everything else in your life staying as it is, the transformation might be less obvious. But it's useful to remember that a change is underway nevertheless.

If you listen to the language of this chatter, it is usually full of absolute statements around who you are ('I'm messy, disorganized, no good at filing...'). It touches on your identity; you might define yourself by it. To question this identity can be daunting and this process is not to be underestimated. But although you might find it difficult to stop doing something, it is far easier to start doing something different instead. So try that!

It can be tricky dismantling beliefs you have been holding on to for a long time, but give it a go. It might not be as hard as you think. You get to decide who you want to be regardless of what box others might have put you into.

Chapter summary

▶ Wanting to own things is natural – but pay attention to how much you have and when it gets too much.

▶ Excessive clutter can create risks in the home: does your clutter enable your efficiency or hinder it?

▶ The 'time to tidy' measure provides a quantifiable way of describing clutter levels in your different spaces.

▶ Wherever possible, keep only those things that make you feel positive.

▶ Suspend your judgmental and critical inner voice; neither is helpful. Decide on a new narrative instead.

3

How clutter affects your life and your relationships

As you've just seen, clutter is about more than excessive stuff that you might keep. Often, this clutter causes all manner of difficulties when you consider the other people in your life, whether they are people you share a living or working space with, or people who have opinions and judgments about your stuff.

Clutter and stress levels

Imagine a desk that is completely covered with stacks of paper, brochures, opened and unopened mail, bills, notebooks, cables, pens, an odd cup or two, and a laptop sitting squarely in the middle of it all. Can you see it in your mind's eye? Is it a desk that you recognize? Maybe your own, or someone else's you know?

That would also be an accurate description of my husband's desk.

I could not work in a space like that, but it doesn't bother my husband enough to want to tidy it. I don't have an answer as to whether he might be more effective or have a clearer mind if his desk was less cluttered, but until he experiences sufficiently painful effects from this space, nothing will make him tidy it, as it is not a problem for him. As for whether it might be a problem for me, the clutter is confined to his office, so it is not in my way!

That said, what we do know from increasing numbers of studies is that clutter affects our stress levels (Saxbe & Repetti 2010, Roster et al 2016). And as we also know, stress has many physiological implications. According to the NHS website (2022), symptoms of stress can include the following:

- **physical symptoms:** headache or dizziness, muscle tension or pain, stomach problems, chest pain or a faster heartbeat, sexual problems
- **mental symptoms:** difficulty concentrating, struggling to make decisions, feeling overwhelmed, constantly worrying, being forgetful
- **changes in behavior:** being irritable and snappy, sleeping too much or too little, eating too much and too little, avoiding certain places or people, drinking or smoking more.

You are probably familiar with the feeling of being stressed. You might attribute it to some obvious sources such as work, people, a busy calendar or daily life. Without closer inspection, you might overlook or not notice the other things that might contribute to those stress levels, such as the physical clutter you're surrounded by.

Of course, when it is for limited time periods and provides you with an adrenaline boost to get something done, some stress can be good. However, when you live with sustained stress levels over long periods of time, it can be damaging. And many of us are increasingly living in a state of permanent stress. What is your current overall stress level? What would you attribute this stress to? Reviewing the list of symptoms above, how many do you experience regularly? And how much might clutter contribute to your stress levels? Noticing the clutter that is in your landscape and removing what is unnecessary can help reduce your stress levels, and the effects might surprise you.

Clutter and relationships

When I tell people what I do, so many of them share their stories about how physical clutter is the source of many arguments in their relationships. Either they are the ones who like to collect, hold on to and treasure all manner of things, or they live or work with someone who clutters up their space. What they all have in common are the arguments that ensue.

How often have you been in an argument with someone about clutter, theirs, yours, or someone else's?

We can have very different preferences, habits and behaviors when it comes to levels of clutter. Some like a neat minimalist space, and others favor a busier environment. And sometimes, a situation is not black or white, one or the other. Some people would like a tidy space but find it difficult to achieve and maintain, and the reasons behind this are often deep rooted and not as obvious as they might think.

One thing is clear: when two individuals have different tidiness preferences and they share the same space, this becomes problematic. Clients regularly come to me and say, 'I like a tidy and organized room, but my partner dumps stuff everywhere. Whenever I clear a bit of space, they fill it right up again and it drives me crazy!' Or they say, 'I'm disorganized and it doesn't bother me, but my partner always complains.'

When you live or work with someone and they have different preferences and clutter tolerance levels, this causes real challenges. It is a significant strain on relationships because it affects you all the time:

- in your home, the place that should be a peaceful and restful sanctuary from the world, and/or
- in the workspace or office, where you are working with others and spend so many hours of your life.

I talked about how clutter in itself causes stress. When this stress is compounded with feelings of animosity toward your partner/family member/housemate/colleague and a close relationship is strained, you suffer even more from the effects of the mess. Your stress levels rise even further, and the associated symptoms become more pronounced.

A study by Saxbe and Repetti from the UCLA Center on the Everyday Lives of Families (CELF) found that people who live in messy and busy homes have higher cortisol levels than those who do not. They also found an interesting additional result: there was a stark difference in how men and women responded to clutter. Generally, women in messy and disorganized homes found them far more stressful than men and had worryingly raised levels of cortisol (Saxbe & Repetti 2010), a hormone that affects, and therefore can disrupt, most of the body's processes (Knezevic et al 2023). This can be useful information if you find yourself in arguments about the tidiness of your home or other shared spaces, and the relative importance of the argument in the first place.

According to the authors, the gender difference can be due to various reasons. Women often tend to take on more of the housekeeping activities, so they see clutter as more work or a reflection on their ability to keep a home. A frequent complaint is also that men simply 'don't see' the clutter and so are blind to the problem. 'Inattentional blindness... demonstrate[s] that salient information can go unnoticed in the absence of attention' (Cohen et al 2012). If no attention is paid to all the stuff lying around, we can simply be blind to it. The process of being conscious of something can happen separately from being aware of something (Pitts et al 2018). We can know that an item is there, but by not giving it any attention, it doesn't filter into our consciousness.

Although this is a gendered challenge, of course it isn't always the case that men are not stressed by clutter, and I have met many men who find mess stressful. It is, however, a point that resonates with many of my clients and workshop attendees, and the key takeaway is simply the difference between individuals.

After a talk I gave on this topic at a financial institution, John came to me and said, 'My wife is always complaining about my messiness, and now I think that I understand why.' A few weeks later he emailed me to proudly share his progress. He had put up some long-awaited shelves and finally unpacked the last set of removal boxes, as well as organized the garage. Not only had he earned brownie points at home, but he also felt a real sense of achievement and put to rest a niggle that he had been carrying around with him.

What effect does clutter have on your relationships? What are the clutter tolerances of everyone in your household or workplace? How significant are the differences?

How the drama triangle can help you break patterns

When we are in conflict with someone, especially when they are close to us, we tend to repeat well-known arguments and patterns. Our fights are familiar, and we can pretty much predict the outcomes. We occupy one or several familiar places on a drama triangle and play out well-rehearsed dialog and emotional states when we have different tolerance levels to clutter than our partner/colleague/housemate. I want to briefly talk about this theory as it can help us improve our interactions with others.

The drama triangle is a model used widely in transactional analysis. It was developed by psychiatrist Stephen Karpman in 1968 and his book *A Game Free Life* (Karpman 2014) covers his follow-on research from the past 50 years in this domain. The model consists of three positions that you find yourself in when you are in a situation of conflict:

- **persecutor:** the critical person who is perceived as the one inflicting harm
- **victim:** the person who is at the receiving end of the persecutor's actions
- **rescuer:** a third party who wants to rescue the victim and/or situation, jumping in to fix the problem out of motivations of their own.

The drama triangle

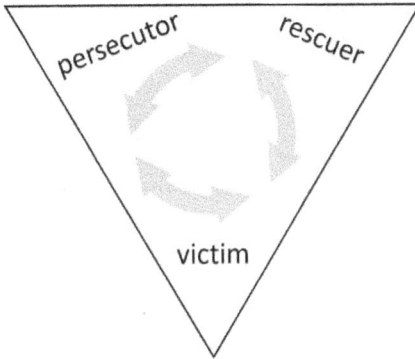

Model by Stephen B Karpman MD (1968)

Here is an example of how these roles in the drama triangle might play out. The person leaving their clutter everywhere might become a persecutor, and the person sharing the space with them could be the victim, suffering increased stress and cortisol levels and feeling resentful. The rescuer could be a third party offering plenty of advice to fix the situation, meaning well but not helping to resolve anything.

In a different scenario, the cluttered person could be the victim and the persecutor the one trying to get them to tidy up, shaming them for their behavior and seeming inability to keep the space organized.

As illustrated by the circular arrows in the diagram, one person can also quickly jump from one role to another without realizing it, each of the positions being a familiar one with a different driver and motivation. As its name suggests, whatever the constellation and distribution of roles, the main thing is that there is drama involved, high emotion, and likely manipulation in some way.

As with any argument, the way out is to acknowledge the situation, identify the roles each person is playing, and to communicate to find a way forward. Following Karpman's work on the drama triangle, a few models were developed to look at moving away from these damaging behaviors and toward a healthier approach to conflict. An example of a winner's triangle is the one developed by Acey Choy (1990), which encourages more helpful attitudes when interacting with each other.

This model replaces the roles from the drama triangle with much healthier positions. Rather than being a victim, someone might admit to feeling **vulnerable**, being truthful about how much they are affected by the mess around them (or by the constant nagging and pressure to tidy up). The persecutor becomes **assertive**, explaining why they leave things where they do (or why they want to see the space being tidied), what about this behavior is important to them, and what they need in this situation. The rescuer becomes a **caring** party, looking to support others and help them resolve conflicts themselves rather than taking over or colluding with either the victim or the persecutor.

When you argue about clutter and have the same discussions over and over again, it can take real effort and energy to step out of your familiar position in the drama triangle and your well-known patterns. But unless you start doing something differently, you will simply perpetuate the same arguments and damage not only your relationship but also your physical and mental health, as well as everyone else around you.

Who do you share physical space with? What patterns are you repeating and how could you shift from the drama to the winner's triangle? What would a healthy conversation around clutter sound like?

Chapter summary

▶ Clutter can affect your stress levels and increased stress can cause many different symptoms.

▶ Clutter impacts men and women differently, with women generally feeling more stressed than men by excessive clutter.

▶ Clutter often causes conflict between people who share a space and have different tolerance levels or preferences.

▶ The drama triangle and its three positions – victim, persecutor and rescuer – is a useful model to help resolve conflict.

▶ Stepping out of the drama of a situation will break your usual patterns and habits around familiar conflict and allow a more constructive conversation.

4

My method for creating physical SPACE

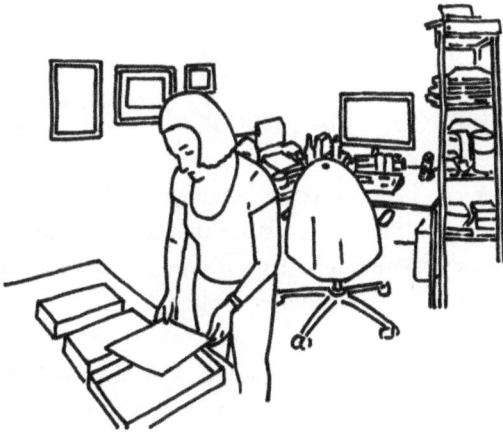

Now that you have spent some time getting to know your clutter, seeing how it can affect you and what impact it might have on your relationships, it is time to do something about it. For this, you will apply the five-step decluttering method introduced in Chapter 1.

Step 1: Survey

The first step in the method is to survey your landscape and look at everything you are dealing with from a place of non-judgmental observation. Once you have a clear picture of what there is to deal with, you can decide what you want to do with it and when.

Let me take you on a tour to give you some thoughts about the different spaces that you might consider adding to your survey. The same principles apply to your home, workplace, office and any other spaces. At the end of the tour, I will talk you through how to document the survey of your own clutter as the starting point for your decluttering exercise.

Tidying: a tour of the house
The office space

Your office can be in an office building, inside your home or somewhere else. It could be a space that is a separate room, or simply an area where you sit down to work, whether at home, in a coworking space or another workplace. It can also be several different places, depending on your working pattern and with whom you are sharing your space. Essentially, I am referring here to where you keep stuff that is related to work, as well as to the running of your house or business.

The type of stuff that my clients tend to find the most difficult to tidy up is paperwork. Now, I call it paperwork, but I am referring to everything that is related to the admin of running your life, and it can be in either a paper or digital format. This would cover things such as bills, bank statements, utility bills, health insurance information, car insurance information and mobile phone contracts and bills.

The sheer volume of all this paperwork can be overwhelming, and the temptation is to put it in a box, physical or digital, and simply ignore it. Thinking back to the metric, what 'time to find' would you feel comfortable with for your desk or office space? What filing system, physical or digital, would you need to achieve this aim? I will cover all things digital in more detail in Chapter 6, but it is useful to consider it here. Remember how everything is interlinked.

In his 2019 book *Indistractable*, author and lecturer Nir Eyal says, 'Removing unnecessary external triggers from our line of sight declutters our workspace and frees the mind to concentrate on what's really important.' He was referring to all the icons on your home screen, but it applies to everything else as well. Examine what is around you when you work and how it affects your focus, attention and effectiveness.

The kitchen

When it comes to decluttering, the kitchen is often overlooked. This can partly be because it is not that clear to see what is simply day-to-day mess, such as dirty dishes, and what is permanent clutter that is in your way. Kitchens are important. As a general rule, they are where you keep and prepare food, even if you might eat it somewhere else. And food is critical to wellbeing. You truly are what you eat, and the difference in how you feel when you eat healthy foods versus unhealthy foods is almost immediately noticeable.

When a kitchen is cluttered and all surfaces are full, using that space is so much more difficult. Also, the smaller the kitchen, the more important it is to pay attention to what is in it that perhaps doesn't need to be there and gets in the way. If your kitchen is in some way a determinant in the food choices you make, then I would suggest taking a close look at it in your survey. And if you are not the person preparing the food in your household, you might like to see how you can support the person who does cook by keeping the kitchen space clear of your clutter.

Is your kitchen a space that you enjoy being in and inspires you to take the time to prepare healthy and nourishing food? Or is it a space where every surface is cluttered and that you really just want to avoid? Of course, food preparation is about having the time to plan and cook as well as having a tidy kitchen, but tidiness might nudge you toward having a functional space when you do want to use it. Taking the time to create a kitchen that you like being in can make a significant difference to your life.

The living space

The living space is where we go to simply be. You might perform some activity there like reading or catching up with social media, or you might relax by consuming some form of entertainment. This is where you rest, you shield yourself from the world, you regenerate, where you can let down the barriers and simply be your true self. Considering the importance of such a space in your home, I feel that it is vital to pay attention to what is around you in this space.

Sarah was a client who loved books but wanted to sort through them to create some space as they were taking over her house. She had recently taken up writing poetry and wanted to add more poetry books to her collection, so room needed to be found for them. As we were working through the shelves in her living room, Sarah came across a set of books that had been with her for many years. They were her PhD books. Picking them up, she shared with me how these books made her feel bad. Every time she looked at them, she was reminded of how she always thought that she should have done more with her PhD. She was in a good job that she enjoyed, had a lifestyle that she loved, and knew she was never going to pursue what she felt that she perhaps *should* do.

After acknowledging that if she ever did want to return to this material, she could find these books in the British Library,

Sarah decided it was time to let them go. Making that decision, then putting them in a box to take away, was hugely liberating for her. There was no need to keep things in her house that made her feel bad.

Thinking back to positive psychology and how it affects us, paying attention to what you keep in your living space matters. Do you want to feel good about yourself or bad about yourself? And what influence does the stuff around you have on these feelings? How many things in your living space are there because you choicefully want them to be there, versus how many are there because they were put there at some point and have stayed where they were set down?

The bedroom

It is easy to overlook the bedroom when decluttering a house, but your bedroom matters hugely because if your living space is where you rest and regenerate, your bedroom is where you sleep. How stressful or restful is your bedroom?

This is the most personal and private space in the home. Rarely, if ever, do we invite visitors to come and view the bedroom, so perhaps you don't pay as much attention to its state as you could. How often is it the last room that you tidy? The last room to receive a fresh coat of paint? The last room where you fix that broken lampshade or that missing piece of baseboard? All these things will create a small cognitive load on your brain, in addition to everything else that you're already carrying.

Sleep affects you as much – albeit differently – if not more than what you eat. Sleep plays a vital part in your health and wellbeing, and as a society we are generally not getting enough of it (Walker 2018). Creating a bedroom that is as restful and calming as possible is crucial to making the most of the hours of sleep that you are getting. Decluttering your bedroom matters.

The wardrobe

I find clothes so interesting. I have always had an interest in fabrics and fashion, and in particular how specific garments make us feel. It is also one of the classic areas that people bring up spontaneously every time I mention decluttering. There will be no surprise here, as clothes are a category of items that are easily accumulated over the years, and we all have varying degrees of difficulty in selecting what to keep and what can be passed on or discarded.

The reason why I have become interested in clothes and decluttering wardrobes is again down to positive psychology, but also to our deeper sense of identity. We have a complex relationship with clothes, and they sit at the intersection of our physical (the bulging wardrobe), mental (thinking about what to wear), and emotional (noticing how we feel in them) clutter.

We all have clothes that we like to wear for different occasions, outfits that will make us feel a particular way: a power suit for an important work meeting, those perfect jeans for going out, the coat that makes us feel fabulous, those old pajamas that feel like a hug. We use our clothes as one or several layers to cover ourselves with, both to protect ourselves and to show what we wish to reveal to the world. Looking into your wardrobe, who are the different selves on those hangers and shelves? Who are you showing to the world? And who are you underneath all the layers?

Of all those clothes in the wardrobe, which ones make you feel good about yourself and which ones don't? There will probably be pieces that don't fit quite right at the moment, or that have hardly ever been worn even though they looked so nice in the shop and cost a lot of money, or that someone else thought suited you but you don't actually like yourself. What do you tell yourself each time you rifle through the closet looking for something to wear? There are endless lists of tips on how to declutter your wardrobe:

- If you haven't worn it for one, three, or x number of years, get rid of it.
- If it doesn't fit, get rid of it.
- If it doesn't go with anything else you own, get rid of it.
- Turn all your hangers back to front. Once a garment is worn, turn the hanger back again so that you can see what has remained untouched. Get rid of it after one, three, or x number of years.
- If it isn't your color (a color that suits your skin tone and makes you look healthy and glowing), get rid of it.

The list goes on.

I would like to suggest keeping only those clothes that make you feel positive in some way (good, happy, confident, fabulous, cozy) and passing on everything else. You can decide how you want to show yourself to the world. Whatever the layers you cover yourself with, how you feel also plays a big part in how others experience you. How you feel shapes your interactions. Your clothes matter.

A great way of making it easier to let go of clothes, especially those that might have cost a lot of money, is to look for the learning in them. What did buying that item teach you about yourself, about what suits you, what you like, what you feel comfortable in? That was the purpose of that item in your wardrobe, not owning it forever.

The garage, shed, attic or other dumping ground
Peter, a colleague who was unhappy in his job and more broadly in his life in general, told me that ideally, he would have liked to move to a different company and a different part of the country,

maybe even abroad. And the thing holding him back? His attic. He had accumulated so much stuff, which he had stored up there, that he simply couldn't face the task of dealing with it. His clutter was keeping him a prisoner in his home. But until we had the conversation that day, he hadn't realized that this was the main thing that was holding him back. Armed with this new awareness, he went away to consider his options for getting unstuck and moving his career and life forward.

When we have space, our natural tendency is to fill it. When it is full, we move to a bigger space. But do we stop and ask ourselves whether this stuff is worth the cost to us of the bigger space? How much is your storage space costing you? A spare room is an expensive option, though we rarely think of it in this way.

If you were to consider the cost of putting all your excessive stuff into a storage unit, would it be worth enough to you to pay for the facility? Sometimes, looking at your landscape from a different viewpoint will give you a different perspective. And if you are holding on to things for someone else, perhaps for children, other family members or friends who might maybe want them someday, it might be worth checking what they are thinking versus what your assumptions might be.

What to do with gifts and heirlooms

I am often asked about what to do with these items, as they usually come loaded with a strong emotional charge and can be difficult to let go of.

Gifts

When you look at the gifts you have received, you might feel that you must hold on to all of them, since passing them on in one way or another would offend the person who gave them to you. Of course, a judgment will be made in relation to the giver and what the item is, and whether passing it on will in any way damage the relationship.

For the majority of cases, I find Marie Kondo's perspective useful. She states that the intention of the gift was to bring joy to the person who gave it to us, and to bring joy to us, the recipient, in the moment when we received it. And at that stage, the item has fulfilled its purpose in our life. This receiving of the item has become a part of who we are and has contributed to shaping our relationship with the giver, and now we don't need the item itself anymore. Sometimes a shift in perspective helps us to feel about and see things differently.

Heirlooms

Decisions about heirlooms are difficult to make because these items are so heavily loaded with meaning. They are about the object, the person it came from, your memories, your feelings, loss, grief, and a whole lot of other things depending on the circumstances. They can be about happy times, sad times, things said, things left unsaid, love, conflict, and so many subtleties that only you yourself feel in your personal landscape of emotions.

The clutter created by heirlooms is a great example of how different types of clutter are interconnected (physical and emotional). In Western cultures, we are not very good at discussing and dealing with death. We feel that to display grief, sorrow or sadness makes us seem weak, and that this is in some way detrimental to our social or professional position. Other countries have more celebratory rituals around the passing of loved ones, and perhaps these can ease some of the pain.

Having a few heirlooms is a wonderful way of staying connected with your past, your family, your roots and your provenance. However, when the space that they take up is simply overwhelming or suffocating, it is time to consider passing on some of the volume. These items all contributed in one way or another to who you are today. In our society, property is important and we like to own stuff. But perhaps the more interesting question is not what you have, but who you are. Acknowledging who you are releases you from needing to hold on to the items themselves.

Sometimes, it can be comforting to hold a small ceremony when letting go of heirlooms. It can be a way of not only finding closure but also giving you permission to start on a new path.

Your turn: surveying your own physical clutter

It is now time to move to action and start your own physical decluttering exercise by completing the first step and creating a survey of your own clutter.

1. Consider all the rooms or areas that you want to tackle.
2. Stand in the doorway of each one of the rooms and simply look at what is there with a cool and detached eye. You are simply taking in data without judgment.
3. From this vantage point, identify all the different types of things in the space. Without any judgment or critical inner chatter, consider where they might belong. Does your office contain sports equipment that belongs in the garage? Does your wardrobe contain books that might belong on shelves? Does your kitchen contain paperwork that belongs in the office?
4. Do this several times, as you might not see everything the first time you look. Standing a few steps removed from the thick of it, get a real sense for what is there.
5. Capture this data in whatever format suits you.

Here is an example of what your physical survey output might look like for your home office:

Area:	home office
Categories of items in the space	
Clothes	
Technical equipment and cables	
Books	
Paperwork	
Tools	
Musical instruments and equipment	
Art supplies	
Spare furniture	
...	

Step 2: Plan

Now that you have surveyed your landscape and broken it down into different areas, you will have a view of your starting point. The next step is to consider what you would like instead, what your ideal is for each space, and this will form the plan of what you want to do.

1. For each of the areas you have identified in the survey step, create a list of all the tasks that need to be done to create the space you desire. These can include:
   - identifying all the items that actually belong in this space
   - removing all the items that don't belong in this space
   - looking at what there might be too much of
   - seeing if something might belong in this space but needs to find a different home due to lack of room.

2. Decide on a time frame within which you want to carry out each of these tasks and prioritize them according to what feels right to you. Remember to check in with yourself around *when* is a good time for you to do these activities.

Continuing with the previous example from Step 1, here is what your plan might look like:

Area:	home office		
Tasks		**Do by**	**Done**
Remove and put away shoes/clothes/bag (don't belong here).		Saturday	✓
Go through old tech items (and cables!) and check what to keep.			
Sort through books and decide which to keep.			
File paperwork.			
Shred/discard paperwork as relevant.			
Tidy desk.			
...			

Step 3: Act

Now that you have a plan, it's time to move to action!

1. Look over the plan that you produced in the previous step and start with the first task today.
2. The key is to get started. Whatever area you decide to deal with first, just start.
3. Some things will be easy to sort out, for example things to put in a recycling box or garbage, so do those first.
4. Then, gather together all the things that belong together (eg all the cables in one box, all the pens in one holder, all the books onto shelves).

5. Decide on what you want to keep and what you can let go of, keeping in mind all the elements from the earlier chapters. Do revisit some of them to refresh your memory.

6. Once you have decided on what you want to keep, look at how much stuff there is and how much space you need and have. Will it all fit?

7. Everything must have a home. Decide where everything will live.

8. Don't aim for perfection – instead, aim for the beginning of a process.

When there is stuff everywhere and the job feels overwhelming, do one thing at a time and stick to it. There will be many temptations to get sidetracked and distracted, so when you notice that happening, bring yourself back to the task you set out on and save everything else for later – for example, reading those old letters again, or looking up something you have come across and want to research.

Joan came to me because she needed help to tidy up a spare room that she wanted to use as an office. There were boxes everywhere across the floor, which had been there since she moved into the house some years earlier. The volume was not overwhelming and there seemed to be enough storage space for everything, so I was curious as to what it was that she found difficult in this process.

It turned out that she had a belief that in order to organize the space, she had to deal with every item inside every box. And one of these boxes contained old photographs from her grandparents. At some point she wanted to put these photographs into albums and thought that a part of the process of clearing and organizing this room meant she had to deal with the photographs and put them into albums.

I suggested she might simply want to put the box of photographs into a cupboard and store them there until she was ready to take care of them. They didn't need to stay on the floor for her to look at and feel bad about all the time, being a job not yet done. Realizing that her boxes and items could be organized and tidied in their current state made a huge difference to Joan. She could address any further activities, such as organizing the photographs into albums, at a later point but still clear her spare room and make the space for an office.

I have come across this stumbling block with various clients over the years, this belief that decluttering means doing everything or nothing. A room can be tidied without every last sheet of paper that needs discarding being shredded. A pile of clothes that need mending doesn't have to be mended to be put away into a box, drawer or cupboard. These tasks can be captured in the plan from Step 2 and can happen at different points in time. Your plan can be as fluid or as rigid as you want it to be, and you can update it whenever you uncover new items or tasks.

Keeping up the motivation

As with any big job that needs to be done over a longer time frame, there can be challenges with motivation. You will have days or times when you feel energized and get plenty done, and other days or times when it is a real struggle to maintain the stamina to carry on.

Here are a few ideas about what could help when you get stuck:

- ◆ Remind yourself continually of your purpose for getting this done now (see Chapter 1).
- ◆ Take the time to repeatedly visualize your spacious and clutter-free result.
- ◆ Project yourself into a future point where you are enjoying this space you have created for yourself.

- Set yourself objectives and hold yourself accountable to them.
- Involve others to help hold you accountable to what you set out to do.

Step 4: Celebrate

It is important to celebrate every little task that you have completed, or even simply started. A decluttering exercise can be a big project with so much to do that an end feels completely out of sight. This is precisely when acknowledging everything you have already done is so important, so that you don't get disheartened by what feels never ending.

1. Spend some time thinking about what a good reward for you would be, identifying how you could celebrate the successes that you achieve throughout this decluttering process.
2. You might have different types of rewards according to the type of activity that you have completed.
3. Find who might be a good person to celebrate with!

Step 5: Evaluate

This final step is all about reflecting on how you are doing and what you can learn from your endeavors. Below are some questions to help you get started with your own personal reflections. You can write some notes or simply mull them over in your head in a quiet moment, as long as you spend a bit of time with some focused thinking.

1. How did the process work for you for this particular task that you performed?
2. What worked well?

3. What didn't work so well?
4. What could you do differently next time?
5. What did you learn about yourself?

To wrap up this final step of the decluttering method, I want to illustrate how valuable the evaluation is by sharing Mandy's story. Mandy had a great emotional attachment to many items from her past and found it difficult to make decisions around letting them go because they all meant so much to her. She was motivated to do the work as she wanted to close an old chapter and begin a new phase. She had decided it was the right time to tackle her stuff, but still she experienced an intense difficulty in letting things go and was not making the progress she was hoping for.

At one point she fell ill, and this illness lasted for a few months. She was struggling to get out of bed and had little energy for anything. But she still decided to carry on, little by little, with her decluttering plan. To her great surprise, she found that it was much easier for her to make decisions around letting things go while she was physically unwell. Her illness had also affected her 'emotional energy' and feelings of attachment to these things from the past. Realizing that the process could be easier at certain times was transformational for Mandy. In her evaluation step, she reflected on how it was for her to do this work when it felt easy, and she held on to that recognition from then on.

Once she became healthy again, she continued with her process of creating physical space. Knowing that she found letting go easier when she was lower in energy, she was able to adjust her plan of when to do what, which made a huge difference to her in moving forward.

Knowing yourself and what works well for you is a real game-changer, and these insights only become conscious when you take the time to reflect. So, although this fifth and final step is the easiest to skip, I invite you to carve out little moments to think. They don't have to take much time out of your schedule: I do a lot of my best thinking lying in bed at night before going to sleep, and when carrying out repetitive tasks such as washing dishes or ironing. Just make sure to focus your mind for some reflection after each decluttering activity.

This completes the final step in the decluttering method, and wraps up Part 1, which covers physical clutter and focuses on creating physical space. I have presented many benefits of decluttering, but there are also costs to not doing it. The costs of staying surrounded by physical clutter might be less obvious, but they are there nonetheless and are worth paying attention to. The world is at saturation point with excessive consumption, and all the while your landscape is overloaded, there is no free space for anything else.

With everything that you remove, every item you tidy away or let go of, you create space to breathe, to think, for some energy for something new to happen. I often talk about the trade-offs we make. These are clear to see in our physical space: when the bookshelf is full and we want to add a new book, an old book needs to be removed. Similarly, when we choose to be cluttered by our old stuff, we are choosing to keep out new stuff. We make these trade-offs all the time, often unknowingly. A part of this decluttering process is also to bring to light the choices that you unconsciously make all the time.

Now let's move on to Part 2, where I look at mental clutter and the trade-offs of carrying too much in our minds.

Chapter summary

- Each area of your home or workspace has a different function and being able to utilize them for their intended purpose will contribute to your overall wellbeing.

- Step 1: Survey your physical landscape by looking carefully at everything in the different areas of your home, workspace or other place you spend time in.

- Step 2: Plan all the tasks that you will carry out to shift from the current state of these spaces to their desired states.

- Step 3: Act by going through your tasks one after the other. Consider your motivation to keep going and put in place strategies to help you when you start flagging.

- Step 4: Celebrate every task that you complete, however big or small. Yes, there is always more to do, but enjoy each small accomplishment to make your progress visible.

- Step 5: Evaluate and be conscious of every learning along the way.

Part 2

Creating mental space

5

Unpacking mental overload

After a brief foray into the production and sales of postcards and greeting cards, my career began in earnest as a graduate trainee in the IT department of a global manufacturing company. This area suited me and my analytical brain, and I ended up spending 16 years in the corporate world.

I learned a lot about IT, of course, but also about business dynamics, leadership, professional identity and mental overload. As I progressed and took on increasing responsibility, my area of operation grew, and with it, the amount of knowledge I needed to hold. Coupled with this expansion, the economic climate was shifting, meaning smaller budgets and increased workload.

Digitization meant that more and more processes were becoming 'self-service', where everyone had to learn to use new platforms for HR services, visitor bookings, travel arrangements and more, which were previously handled through an email or a phone call.

Some of these shifts were big, some of them minor, but all of them gradual and stretching an already saturated mind. This is when I became interested in mental clutter: how much we carry, where it comes from, how it affects our efficiency, our work and our quality of life outside of work.

Everyone I talk to is busy. There is an epidemic of overload and burnout, which have such devastating effects on people. Not only does it take a long time to recover physically from burnout, but it also often leaves people with a feeling of diminished confidence and self-esteem. The signs will have been there long before the final collapse, but they are so often pushed aside for many reasons, because of the many stories we're telling ourselves around what it means to be unable to cope.

Part 2 looks at these stories, all of this clutter that we generate, process and carry in our minds. At the end, I'll go through the decluttering method again so you can see how you can clear some of that mental clutter and create more headspace.

Understanding mental clutter

These days, it might seem as if you are always switched on. You go from one thing to another, often so quickly that you trick yourself into believing you're multitasking, and you get to the end of the day without having caught your breath. The world has become increasingly complex on so many levels, and you are having to process more and more information simply to get through everyday tasks. And that puts a strain on the brain, which has to constantly process all this information.

After one talk I gave at a bank, one attendee came up to me and said, 'I don't have a cluttered desk, or office, or home, so I didn't think I'd be interested in the topic of decluttering. But now I realize that I am holding everything in my head. I thought that was normal, and I hadn't noticed how draining it is.'

With physical clutter, it is easy to see what is around you, in your landscape, in your life. You can readily see the volume of what you have and how much physical space it occupies. When it comes to what is in your mind, however, it is less easy to see. And because you don't see it, you are less aware of the amount of it and how much it might impact you.

We each experience too much mental clutter differently. When I feel overwhelmed, I notice that my brain isn't functioning very well anymore. Everything seems that much more difficult. I am slower at processing information. Often I have to read the same thing over and over again before it goes in, and my temper is short. If I am in a high-pressure situation, adrenaline will keep me going and allow my brain to continue to function, but it will be exhausting. I will then go to bed with all this stuff whirling around in my mind, and it will keep me awake even though I sorely need the rest. Then an unhealthy caffeine intake cycle kicks in to cope with the tiredness, making everything worse.

You often might not realize how, one after another, big and small things that need your attention creep into your life. You don't notice how your mental capacity is filling up, how all the stuff slowly snowballs into something that is huge and all consuming and that you didn't see coming.

The expression 'the straw that broke the camel's back' comes to mind. A piece of straw in itself is so light that you couldn't possibly imagine how it could break anything! But at some point, too much is too much. And it is the same for you. You might have a complete meltdown simply because you are asked a simple question: would you like hot or cold milk with your coffee? Because at that point, you are already holding and processing so much stuff that you have no further mental capacity to make even a simple decision. So you lose your temper and shout that you don't care what temperature the milk is, you simply want a white coffee!

In those moments, you know that you are not being rational anymore. This is an extreme situation, a manifestation of feeling totally overwhelmed. You can lose a significant amount of effectiveness way before this point, and in the following chapters I will explore some areas that require your brain function, sometimes without you even noticing them. By paying attention to these things, you can shine a light on them in order to make choices about how you want to let them affect you.

What are the symptoms that indicate that you are feeling overwhelmed? What are the signs slightly ahead of time that could indicate that you are heading toward that state? How does your mental clutter affect you at the moment?

Different ways of looking at overwhelm

When I began my research into mental clutter, one of the ways in which I tried to look at it was from the perspective of external versus internal clutter. I felt that mental clutter could either come from external sources, such as all the emails in our inbox, the information overload when it comes to consuming news, researching all the details before booking a holiday, or our work projects and pressures. On the other hand, mental clutter could also come from internal sources, such as our own belief systems, values and drivers. But the more I tried to apply this classification, the more I concluded that it didn't give a full picture.

What I found instead was that the extent to which our mental clutter affects us is a combination of both. We can't differentiate between them because what we are dealing with is effectively how our internal stories and beliefs process the external clutter coming in at any given point in time.

So, the fact that you might be struggling with the number of emails in your inbox won't simply be down to how many unread emails you have and who sent them, but rather how you feel about them and what you think you should be doing with them. It will be your belief that emails require responses, or a value that you hold that says it is important to be responsive and reply to messages immediately, which will lead to a build-up of stress.

Someone else might have the same number of unread emails, but these might not affect them as much because they hold the different belief that they are the master of their own time and they determine if and when they will respond, rather than feel any pressure from the outside. How much you are affected by external stuff is pretty much down to your internal stuff. And that makes it that bit more difficult to untangle.

Another factor that has an effect on how much your mental clutter can get in your way is the 'straw effect' described above. It isn't one particular thing that causes a problem, but rather an accumulation of all manner of things that can make you reach breaking point. You might find yourself being short tempered in a meeting with a difficult colleague. You know them and are usually able to smoothly navigate the challenges that they might make you face. After a conversation with them has not gone as well as you had hoped, you can either doubt your abilities and professionalism or notice instead all the other mental clutter that had accumulated and you were holding in that moment. The latter is a much more useful insight to learn from.

To put an additional layer on top of your mental clutter, how you feel brings in your emotions, and as you know, these can also be complex little (or big!) things. Part 3 on creating emotional space looks at emotional clutter in more detail, but I also want to mention it here because our emotions are inextricably linked to how we are in the world and how we respond to situations. They are useful signposts and can also be helpful in identifying the state we are getting into or are already in. What emotions are signposts for you that you are reaching a tipping point around your mental capacity?

Keeping up with modern living

Last year, my local council changed how they manage permits for residents' on-street parking. Until then, residents could apply for an annual parking permit for the part of town they lived in and receive a sticker to go on the windscreen. Residents could also apply for and purchase a certain number of visitors' permits, in the form of paper vouchers on which you could write the date and vehicle registration. It was an easy process, for both the residents and the parking wardens checking the cars.

We now have a new digital, automated system. Parking permits are paid for online and the details are stored in a computer system. The windscreen sticker is no more. Similarly for visitors' permits, these are now purchased online and the car registration number is inputted electronically. There are no more paper vouchers. Parking wardens carry electronic devices with which they scan the license plates of parked cars, and the computer says either yes or no.

Of course, this new system is meant to be more efficient, more reliable and save taxpayers money. Maybe for some parties involved, it achieves some of this desired increased efficiency. But for the residents and their visitors, this new system is yet another website to navigate, another account to create, another password to remember, and countless phone calls to make when technological blips mean the registration numbers have not been updated correctly on the warden's device and another ticket has been issued incorrectly. This is one example among so many of how our world is becoming more and more demanding for our brains to navigate. Everywhere we look, services are being automated and processes introduced to supposedly make it simpler and cheaper for companies to run their business, or for local authorities to deliver their services.

I am certainly not against technology as a whole, but the introduction of digital solutions often comes at a cost to the users and consumers. In some cases, you have a choice about whether you want to purchase a product or service. If you are not in the mood or don't have the mental capacity to engage with a new website or app, you can leave it for another time when you do have the energy. In many other cases, however, you don't have a choice and have to engage with new ways of doing things. This is happening all the time, and at an increasingly faster pace. Do you enjoy and embrace new technology or different ways of doing things? Or do these things drain you?

So why does it all matter? It matters because simply running your life and your household is becoming more and more demanding on your brain. There are several terms that have been coined over the past few years to describe this. 'Digital housework' relates to all the tech activities you need to carry out to run your household or family. 'Shadow work' encompasses all the activities that are now pushed onto the consumer/resident/patient that used to be carried out by other people as a part of a process or service. In the name of modernization and cost cutting, we are now at the receiving end of much work that has been pushed down the line.

And that's before you even start thinking about your actual job and all the demands on your brain that doing good work might require, or the different ways in which you might communicate with your friends, clients and colleagues on a multitude of platforms. Trying to remember where you saw a particular message that still needs a reply, or where you might find that piece of information again, is exhausting.

Keeping up with everything is a job in itself, and little slips along the way like a forgotten message or meeting here and there can make you doubt your ability to function well in the world. You start judging yourself and creating a heap of negative self-talk, all the while not noticing that your environment is hugely demanding, to such an extent that your human brain was not designed to be able to handle.

The world is complex, changing at ever-faster speed, and it is no surprise if you feel as if you're not always on top of everything anymore. We take our brains for granted, but our mental capacity, our brain processing power, is not unlimited. It is finite.

Your brain and its processing power

The human brain is amazing! Research into understanding how it works continues to keep scientists from many diverse disciplines busy, and new findings emerge regularly. The part of the brain that I want to mention here is the prefrontal cortex. It is the part of the brain that carries out the executive function, where all our daytime processing takes place. It is where we take in information and make decisions based on goals and preferences, make judgments on whether something is good or bad, and where we work out the consequences of our choices. This is essentially the machine room that allows us to function and drives our actions, and the area that feels the overwhelm when it is overloaded.

This part of the brain, the prefrontal cortex, has a finite amount of processing power. It can only handle so many processes at any one time, and even if it is impressive in its abilities, it is nonetheless limited. In his book *The Organized Mind* (2014), neuroscientist Daniel Levitin says: 'Every status update you read on Facebook, every tweet or text message you get from a friend, is competing for resources in your brain with important things like whether to put your savings in stocks or bonds, or how to best reconcile with a close friend you just had an argument with.'

These words struck a chord with me and I find them to be a good illustration of what our brains are faced with in our modern world. We live in an age of information overload, stimulus overload, addiction-inducing distracting social media platforms, and a general sense of never quite being in control of all the plates we are juggling. Simply dealing with your day-to-day life creates so much mental noise that it can make it difficult to stay focused on any one activity or task.

Add to that a speeding up of everything around us, from the immediacy of news feeds to the near-immediacy of online shopping deliveries, to an on-demand entertainment industry at our fingertips, leading us to being switched on and alert at all times. Our modern world has made thinking, reflecting and mental processing time almost nonexistent. So it's no wonder if you feel frazzled most of the time and frustrated by a feeling of lack of control over your life.

Coming back to your brain processing power and how you utilize it, mindless distractions are so readily available and enticing when things get hard that it is easy to glide through the days with a sense of lost agency. And as a result, more often than not, you successfully avoid the big and meaningful stuff and still have the illusion that you have been 'busy'. Where you might notice the habits and distractions in others, you might not always see your own.

Reclaiming your agency over your mental processing power is essential for your wellbeing and effectiveness, both in the workplace and your personal life. What tends to take up most of your mental processing power? What is the big stuff that you are not getting around to at the moment? What do you notice or know about your tendencies to become distracted?

Let's take it to the bedroom

Another interesting thing about our prefrontal cortex is that to function well, it has some clever cleansing and resetting routines. After a day's work, it clears down its processors and resets itself for the next day – routines that take place while you sleep (Killgore 2010). But this is not all that happens in your brain when you sleep. Alongside resetting the prefrontal cortex, other parts of the brain also kick in.

Sleep is when your brain works through the information you take in during the day to form memories and store them away where you can retrieve them later. It is also when you process difficult emotions and emotional regulation takes place. I will talk about this in more detail in Part 3. Sleep helps you organize your mental clutter so that you can make sense of it, rather than having it overwhelm you (Eugene & Masiak 2015).

Sleep is also vital to the healthy functioning of the body and mind for so many other reasons. We are seeing increasing amounts of research into the field of sleep and the effect it has on us. There is still a lot that we don't understand, but we are getting a much better picture of why sleep is important. Our bodies repair themselves while we sleep; sleep heals whichever area of our body needs it; it regenerates our cells and is our body's natural painkiller (Walker 2018).

It is clear that we need to take sleep seriously. Nowadays, sleep is so often considered a luxury, with difficulties in both going to sleep and staying asleep becoming the norm and affecting more and more people. As a society, we are chronically sleep deprived. We spend our days overstimulated by a deluge of information, interactions and other distractions, so that when it comes to bedtime, we find it difficult to still our minds and go to sleep.

We are also battling against big marketing budgets, with entertainment companies trying to engage us for as long a time as possible. Back in 2017, in an interview presenting Q1 results to analysts, Netflix CEO Reed Hastings famously stated that Netflix was 'competing with sleep' (Raphael 2017). Your waking hours have been commodified! Since then, online entertainment platforms have continued to grow, encroaching ever more on our rest time.

Add to that the social stigma of admitting that you are tired and need a nap to function at your best, and it is easy to forget what it feels like to be well rested. When you wake up after a good night's sleep, you have energy, you feel optimistic and look forward to the day. You are productive, you follow through on your plans, you are aware and mindful of others, and your world feels expanded.

At the opposite end, you are probably also familiar with what it feels like to wake up after a short or bad night's sleep. Everything is that little bit more difficult. You are slower to get your body moving, your brain feels slightly foggy, your thinking is more sluggish and you make unhealthier food and drink choices, feeding a downward spiral. You have less time for others and prefer to retreat into yourself. Effectively, this is the trade-off for watching that next episode that auto started. Tip: You can turn off that feature!

There are a multitude of tips available for having a good bedtime routine: for example, avoiding all screens anything between 30 minutes and two hours before going to bed; sticking to a set bedtime every night; or using meditation, journaling or other practices to calm the mind.

As already mentioned in Chapter 4, the space where you go to rest also affects how well you sleep. If your bedroom is messy or stressful in other ways, this can impact on the quality of your sleep too. But probably one of the biggest disruptors of sleep is all things digital, which is what I will look at next.

Chapter summary

▶ It's easy to overlook the heavy strain on the brain created by a constant stream of data, information, newsfeeds and processes that need to be navigated every day.

▶ Your brain gets cluttered not only by all this data coming from the outside world, but also by your internal narratives, beliefs and judgments.

▶ Simply keeping on top of modern living can be exhausting, with many administrative tasks now being done via digital processes and requiring more effort to navigate.

▶ Your brain has a finite amount of processing power, so there is always a trade-off in where you choose to put your attention.

▶ Sleep is essential to keep your brain functioning well. Sacrificing sleep is never a good long-term solution.

6

Living in the digital age

Although I've already touched on technology, I want to expand on it here because it affects so much of our lives. Technology has a huge impact on our brains, what we think about, how we communicate with others, how we work and how we lead our daily lives.

Everything around us is becoming digitized. Technology is not only everywhere you look, it is also where you don't see it and is developing at breathtaking speed. Collectively, we produce more data daily than we could ever imagine, and we store all this data somewhere. Then, we use various tools and apps to perform more and more of our daily activities. Staying on top of all these tools also requires a lot of our energy.

The digital data that we create

The latest estimate for the amount of digital data created in 2024 is 149 zettabytes (Statista 2024). Do you have any idea about what that represents? This number is bigger than anything our brains are able to comprehend or make sense of (the number of bytes – units of digital information – in a zettabyte is 1 followed by 21 zeroes). The amount of stuff in our digital sphere is simply too vast and overwhelming, and with the explosion of generative AI, the volume of data produced has grown exponentially to an even more gigantic scale. It is endless in comparison to what our brains might be able to process.

You may already be aware of these overwhelming volumes when you consider the data that you create digitally: files, photos, videos, emails, web browser bookmarks, screenshots and more. This data is intangible: you can't see the stacks pile up on your desk, on the floor, in photo albums, on your DVD shelves, so it doesn't register as clutter. But it is there, and you will carry it to a greater or lesser extent in your awareness.

With memory space now so cheap to purchase and with files stored in a seemingly magical 'cloud', we are no longer restricted by space and therefore merrily accumulate without feeling the need to delete what is obsolete. Quite the opposite! It is so easy to copy files that we might well hold multiple versions of the same thing. This all comes at a cost – a cost to us, but also a heavy cost to the environment.

It is worth stopping to notice how much your digital data does clutter your mind, especially if you don't have a good filing system that allows you to have an overview of what you've saved and where to find it. Creating a good filing system online for all this stuff is just as important as having a well-organized physical filing cabinet in your office. Because simply knowing that all this clutter is there, in a mess, and not knowing where to find things, is a huge stressor.

On the upside, we can also use technology to help us navigate the volumes of data, as there is often a helpful 'search' function, when we know what word(s) to search for. For some, that can work well. For others, the thought of the mess of files can be completely overwhelming. In certain cases, it can also result in having to redo work because of files that were saved somewhere and couldn't be found again.

The digital data that we consume

Alongside the data that we create ourselves, we are also permanently confronted with vast quantities of data and information that is directed our way. Whether it is in the form of newsfeeds, newsletters, emails, internal communications at work, messaging on all manner of platforms, the information overload is constant and it impairs our ability to process data meaningfully.

When I first came across the term 'infobesity', another term for information overload, I found that it touched on the challenge that too much data creates in an almost visceral manner. It gives the sense of an epidemic and attaches a health connotation, which we might not think about when we simply talk about too much information, but the health implications are real. Data overload can lead to stress, anxiety and fatigue, and result in poor decision making and lost effectiveness. In handling this volume of information, your brain is effectively going into what it thinks is multitasking mode but is in fact a constant switching between tasks. And this activity is highly energy intensive as well as addictive. It's exhausting and unproductive (Levitin 2015).

'It's not information overload. It's filter failure' (Shirky 2008). This is a line that immediately struck a chord when I came across it and it has stayed with me ever since. This view allows us to see where we can take control again, where we can decide what we want to see, as well as how much of it, rather than being bombarded against our will.

There are many ways of taking back this control, from using tools to limit your time on various platforms, to being ruthless in deciding what you give your attention to. What it all boils down to is:

1. noticing your behavior
2. taking a step back and seeing your patterns
3. recognizing that we live in an era in which we are manipulated by attention-seeking technologies
4. determining for yourself what you want to spend your valuable brain processing power on.

The tech tools that we use

Alongside all our files, photos and emails, there are also all the applications that we use. Everything we do now seems to involve downloading and engaging through an app or website of some sort (doctor's surgery, library, supermarket, airlines, conferences, booking meeting rooms). Some will be useful and used regularly; others will simply accumulate on our devices, homepages and sidebars. All this clutter causes distraction and creates a load on our brains (Eyal 2019).

In the same way as with your digital data, digital tools also need a regular review and clear-out to remove what is unnecessary and impairs your focus. How many apps do you have on your phone? How many icons are on your screen that you never use? When I get a new phone, I systematically go through what is installed by default and remove everything I don't want or need. Everything that is in your line of sight will create a cognitive load. Having to ignore all the apps that you don't want will take effort.

Finally, I want to mention sustainability here too because that aspect is completely invisible to us when we use our devices. Every little thing that you do on your phone will send the data centers whirring and use power. Taking a quick picture, putting a reminder on your phone, adding an item to an online shopping list, reading an email, scrolling on your platform of choice, every little thing you do requires energy in an invisible warehouse in a far-flung location. This cost is conveniently out of sight, but it is there nonetheless.

Let's talk about social media

We all have different thoughts and feelings about social media and the different platforms that fall under this heading. You might enjoy the connectedness they enable by easily keeping in touch with friends and relatives, see them as a tool for finding out what is happening in your local area, or like reading or watching what your peers or favorite celebrities are up to. On another level, you might dislike the manipulation and curation of your newsfeed, or feel obliged to use these tools for your business when you would rather not engage with them, and they become a source of pressure and stress. All these thoughts are valid and useful to be aware of.

To add to this, I also want to highlight the design features that affect our usage behaviors. By that, I mean how addictive these tools are and how their distracting features can affect your focus and productivity. A lot of research has emerged over the past few years that demonstrates how the likes of Facebook, X/Twitter, Instagram and other platforms have teams of designers tasked with making their products as engaging and as addictive as possible (Mujica et al 2022, Esposito & Ferreira 2024). Their main business aim is to maximize 'user engagement'.

A key design feature is, of course, the 'notification', using sound and the color red for maximum noticeability. It is meant to remind you to use a social media platform in case you happen to look away for a moment. These notifications are designed to attract your attention immediately and distract you from whatever other comparatively unimportant task (in the view of the businesses behind the platform, of course) you might have been doing. And they feed our need for love and validation, tapping into our most basic human instincts.

Once you have been successfully lured onto the apps, you are then encouraged to stay on them for as much time as possible. Enter the second design feature: the infinite scroll. Before its introduction, data was presented in pages. When you reached the end of the page, you clicked to load the next one (Google results, for example, are still presented in this way). Offering you endless information through a bottomless scroll feature has effectively removed your natural cue to stop and consider whether you want to continue. Design engineer Aza Raskin, who introduced this feature for a more 'seamless user experience', estimates that an equivalent of 200,000 human lifetimes is wasted on a daily basis due to the act of infinite scrolling. That's a lot! In a tweet posted on 11 June 2019, he said: 'One of my lessons from infinite scroll: that optimizing something for ease-of-use does not mean best for the user or humanity.'

So, why does this matter? It matters from the perspective of brain capacity, effectiveness and focus. Of course, taking a break and choosing to spend a set amount of time catching up on your newsfeed is not a problem. However, realizing that you spent one hour scrolling instead of ten minutes starts to become a problem. How much is technology distracting you? What are your behavior patterns around social media usage? How much agency do you feel you have when you are online and engaging with these apps? Perhaps consider switching off all the notifications, asking a teenager or someone in a phone shop to help you if you don't know how to do it yourself. At work, your IT department could also be a useful resource to help you customize your various applications so that they work for you.

Being mindful of the finite amount of brain processing power you have, all the while you are cluttering up your brain with content that you are being force-fed in huge volumes, you are not thinking about the big stuff in your life, and you have no capacity to make it happen. Some early designers and engineers of these platforms are now speaking out about the long-term unintended consequences of the features they helped develop. Tristan Harris, previously design ethicist at Google and now co-founder of the Center for Humane Technology, is particularly active and vocal in calling out the harm that some of these features can do.

The attention economy

It is not only social media platforms that are trying to steal your attention. We now live in a world where our attention is a commodity, and trying to safeguard it can be an uphill struggle (Williams 2020). Last year, while traveling on a highway in Germany, I stopped at a service station and used the bathroom. When I came to wash my hands, in front of me was a large mirror. The bottom half of this mirror was a screen showing ads on a loop. Businesses followed me all the way into the toilets to try and sell to me!

When you start looking around, you'll notice more and more space that is taken up by advertising. What used to be static billboards are now replaced by screens, with their brightness and moving images attracting the eye constantly in places such as building frontages, shop windows, taxis, hospital waiting rooms and along subway escalators. Our attention is stolen from us everywhere, all the time (Wu 2017). This comes at a great cost to us as individuals, as it interferes with our agency and ability to pursue our own goals, and to us as a society. If businesses are willing to spend that kind of budget on distracting us, our attention must be of great value.

It is easy to overlook the value of your attention, as you take it for granted. You think you're in control of where your mind meanders, but often you're not. You are being distracted at every turn. Of course, you might not be interested in any of the products or services flung at you, but you are being robbed of your focus. These constant bright and, depending on the location, also noisy interruptions to your thoughts mean that it can be difficult to find quiet thinking time while you go about your life.

When you are dealing with your own device, you can choose to switch it off. When your senses are assaulted by giant screens around you, it is more difficult to block them out. But the starting point is always to notice your landscape and pay attention to what is around you, and less distracting routes or noise-canceling headphones can help you protect your attention. If your attention is a commodity that is worth big money and your attention is exactly what many businesses are trying to attract, you also need to start treating your attention as something valuable and guard it fiercely.

Chapter summary

▶ Like your paper files, your digital data also needs a good filing system.

▶ Even if you can't physically see the stacks of photos and DVDs around you, this data still exists digitally and takes up space, both in data centers and in your mind.

▶ Be conscious of the amount of digital data you consume and be choiceful around what you want to let through your filters.

▶ Remove from your devices all the apps you do not need or want. Do not let the manufacturer's default clutter your screens.

▶ Turn off all the notifications that you do not need from the various apps on your phone and computer.

▶ Be mindful of the powerful manipulative techniques used by social media and other platforms and decide how much time you want to spend on them.

▶ Protect your attention fiercely from all the insidious distractions around you.

7

Managing your busyness

'Hello, I haven't seen you for a long time. How are things?'

'Yes, it's been a while! Things are really busy. It's somehow even busier than before, though that hardly seems possible.'

Does this sound familiar? I hear it a lot, both in a professional and personal context. We constantly seem to be at capacity, or somewhere beyond capacity, most of the time. And somehow, from one year to the next, our busyness still ramps up. It has been an ongoing trend for at least a decade and is not slowing down – quite the opposite, in fact. 'Being busy' has become a badge of honor and it can also become blended with our identity.

Work—life or life—work balance?

We spend a huge amount of our time at work, and whatever the circumstances – whether you are employed full time, part time, working for yourself, or have a portfolio career – work can be both fulfilling and a source of pressure and stress.

You might have too much work, too little work, too many demands from others, difficult colleagues, difficult clients… Even when you love your job, it consumes a huge amount of your mental capacity. Add to that the technology that is now commonplace, the hyper-connectivity, the tendency to be always switched on, and your beliefs around being available and responsive. Even if you are disciplined and vigilant around your boundaries, how regularly do you send that quick email out of hours, reply to that message?

You might also use the same device for your work and your personal life, so even when you are not working but chatting with friends and family, you can still be interrupted and distracted by work-related emails and messages.

Workplaces have also shifted to working much more from home, and this has had a huge impact on many people's lives. In addition to what I mentioned in Chapter 4 about our physical workspace, working from home also means no commute to help you get ready for the day in the morning, and to mentally process and close the day in the evening.

This way of working also brings with it tremendous opportunities and flexibility, allowing us to work in a way that suits us rather than following the rigid guidelines of an office. It certainly isn't all bad! But there is no longer always a clear spatial separation between our working life and our personal life, making it incredibly difficult to set and keep mental boundaries.

Maybe when you are working, you see dishes in the sink or the lawn that needs mowing. And when you are cooking dinner or playing with the children, you are thinking about the email that needs a response and the blog you were going to write. The lines are so blurred that they have almost disappeared.

So what can you do when it feels as if work has become all consuming? You notice that the scales have tipped too far. You pay attention to your habits and recognize that to stay effective and productive, you need to find a balance. You need to find ways to switch off and recharge, not only physically but also mentally. Set yourself spacial boundaries around where you work, time boundaries for when you are available, mental boundaries for when you will stop thinking about work and focus on something else instead, and find rituals to perform at the end of each day to switch off and give your mind a rest.

The creep to ever-more

I can think back to a time when 9 am to 5 pm was considered normal working hours for office workers. I remember working that schedule for a while when I was fairly junior and then, slowly, those hours extended. A meeting might be scheduled for 9 am, so I would arrive at 8.30 am to be ready for the 9 am start. My calendar would fill up during the day, meaning that I would only get started with going through my emails at 5 pm, effectively extending my working day until 6 pm or 7 pm. What surprises me now is how quickly that became a new normal.

This trend of extending working days far beyond what could be considered reasonable is one that I see with pretty much all my clients, and it is something that they all struggle with. There is simply too much to do and there are not enough hours in the day, so workdays are stretched as far as they can go, usually with a sleep deficit as a result. And this is now considered the new habit, the new normal.

Businesses, public services and organizations are under incredible pressure to deliver services and profits, especially in the current economic climate. Over the years, budgets have been whittled down again and again, leaving staff to deliver increasingly more with ever-shrinking resources – both financial and human – more and more quickly. And this in an age when our life admin is also becoming increasingly demanding. Modern living means many people are at saturation point, often spinning dozens of plates at once, and a small hiccup can make them all come crashing down.

This takes its toll. A 2023 estimate puts the cost to the UK economy of work-related stress and burnout at £28 bn a year (AXA 2023). Burnout and mental ill health are on a steady rise, costing employers and their staff dearly. For employees, the cost is not only their mental health but also their physical health, their relationships, and the ripple effects on their colleagues, family and friends (Nekoei et al 2024).

In this context, work is all consuming and it can feel impossible to have the headspace to consider the bigger themes of your life. How do you focus on your vision, at work or at home, when your time and energy are spent firefighting every day and simply keeping going without falling off the treadmill?

It is time to look at what habits you might have developed and what choices are available to you. You might feel that your workload is out of your control and that everything simply needs to be done, but I would like to challenge that assumption. Here are a few strategies that might help you, though there will be many others. Play around with them and see what sticks:

- Review all your commitments and check that you are in fact required. Every time I ask one of my clients to remove three meetings from their calendar, they are able to do it with surprising ease.
- Block out time in your calendar when you are unavailable for meetings.
- The number of emails/messages you receive is directly

proportionate to the number of emails/messages you send, so think more carefully before you hit 'reply', or even worse the dreaded 'reply all'! Perhaps phone calls need to make a comeback.

◆ If you feel overloaded, reframe your activities by considering the worst thing that could happen if you did not perform certain tasks.

◆ Determine what you would like your normal working hours/days to be and actively work toward making that happen rather than letting the volume creep up unchecked.

Many of these strategies will require a shift away from your current habits, and this can be tricky if your current habits of being busy are linked to your identity and your view of who you are.

When being busy is who you are

Your brain can play games with you. It has grown into your own personalized supercomputer, and its main aim is to keep you safe. One way it has of doing this is by initially resisting anything that is new or unfamiliar. If your typical way of being is to constantly rush from one thing to the next and feel harassed much of the time, any deviation from that will be unfamiliar and new. And sometimes, for some people, that might be a frightening place – a place they are actively avoiding.

Your identity might have become tied in with 'keeping busy', and being anything else might feel scary. Who would you be if you were not busy? What might you need to confront if you weren't sidetracked by emails? Filling up your mind with all manner of distractions and clutter can be an effective way of avoiding that question.

Katja came to me because she had reached breaking point. She was on a treadmill, working a busy job and running a charity alongside it. Her mind was so cluttered that she felt overwhelmed all the time. This was not a state that she enjoyed, and she knew that something had to change, but was also terrified about what might happen if she slowed down and gave herself the space to think. She didn't have a sense of who she was if she wasn't working all the time and was fearful of what she might find if she were to look under the surface.

In our work together, Katja uncovered many layers of beliefs about herself and her worth, and dismantled some thought frameworks she had constructed in her youth and that were no longer serving her. She successfully reached her goal: the ability to appreciate holidays, be present with her partner and have the headspace to enjoy reading a book again for the first time in years. And then came another breakthrough. This headspace she had created allowed other memories to rise to her consciousness. She was now able to face, voice and process traumatic abuse she had suffered as a child. She hadn't realized that this was at the core of all her running and keeping busy, and finally allowing herself to acknowledge and accept her past gave her a huge sense of peace.

Keeping yourself cluttered is a fail-safe way of evading a deeper exploration of who you are, dealing with difficult situations, or pursuing something new. While you are at capacity with one thing or another, or perhaps a deluge of things, you have no space for anything new. You have no ability to move to something else because your clutter is keeping you right where you are.

A big part of this exercise is to be truthful with yourself, and that can be scary and tough. Again, timing is important. You are not always resourced to deal with the tricky stuff, and that's

OK. Simply be aware if you are avoiding something because it's difficult, even if it is hard to admit this to yourself. It's fine if you are happy where you are. But if you are not, then it might be time to clear some space for something else, when the time is right.

Simplify, simplify, simplify!

This is a mantra that I repeat to myself regularly and mention every time I give a keynote or run a workshop.

I spoke earlier about information overload and how the constant stream of data and information can take its toll on your ability to think. I also looked at the complexity of modern lives and jobs, which require a vast amount of brain processing power simply to keep on top of things. This all comes at a cost, and there is a trade-off in everything that you do.

I love learning new things and making new connections with interesting people. But I also realize that for me to focus on writing this book and completing it, I need to give it my attention and brain processing power. Right now, I am actively filtering out a whole set of data and information that I am choosing not to engage with at the moment, such as non-urgent emails in my inbox, newsletters I enjoy reading, event invitations, or books I would like to read. I am increasingly noticing that I need more space in my life, so I am becoming more and more active in determining what I allow into my landscape.

Honing your filters is also a positive way of thinking about how you can take control of what you allow into your brain space. Are there certain people in your life who generate mental clutter and drain you of energy, whom you might reduce your exposure to for a while? Or could you choose to shop in a small supermarket rather than a superstore, not only speeding up your shopping trip but also giving your brain a break from taking in and distinguishing between the thousands of items on the shelves? Could you decide on a whole collection of items on your to-do list and classify them as 'will not be done' or 'will be done next year'?

I would also push this a little further and suggest that when something new comes up, instead of asking yourself 'How can I fit this in?', instead go for 'Do I want to fit this in?' And if the answer is yes, 'What will I stop doing to make this work?'

It can be liberating to actively choose not to do something without feeling bad about it. That might be easier said than done but honing your 'saying no gracefully' muscle will be so rewarding in the long run. In order to experiment with using this muscle, you might also consider decluttering some beliefs and assumptions you are carrying, as well as those values that might have been useful in the past but don't serve you anymore. Do you tend to be a people pleaser? Or do you carry a belief that people will stop loving you if you don't do something they ask you to do?

Finally, being realistic is also key to a simpler and more spacious life. We tend to *overestimate* what we can achieve in the short term, and *underestimate* what we can achieve in the long term (Newport 2024). Tasks always take longer than we think, and yet we continue to overstuff our to-do lists and then feel bad about not achieving as much as we had hoped. Let's give ourselves the time to do things well.

Chapter summary

► Life doesn't have to be ruled by work, even if it seems that way at the moment.

► Set boundaries to create space for personal time and life, readjusting the scales when needed.

► Beware of the creep to more and more, and actively choose what you want your typical working day to look like.

► Be truthful with yourself and look at how much you thrive on being always busy, how much the rushing around is tied into who you think you are.

► Actively simplify everything in your life as much as you can, and it might be more than you think.

8

My method for creating mental SPACE

Now that you have identified some of the mental clutter that you might be carrying and perhaps weren't aware of, let's look at clearing some of it. Again, apply the five-step decluttering method described in Chapter 1.

Step 1: Survey

The first step of the decluttering process is to survey your inner landscape. When your thoughts keep multiplying and spinning around, you might experience a loss of control. You might no longer know what is there, how much of it there is, what is buried in the depths, or even how to start making sense of it. You get distracted by the various strands in your mind, follow one for a while and then jump onto the next one, or avoid them altogether with distractions. It becomes more difficult to get things done and the overall bigger picture gets lost.

One reason why a career in IT suited me well is because it allowed me to use and hone my analytical skills, which I now regularly use in my coaching work. In listening to my clients, I can hear their often-tangled stories and threads of thought and can help them sort these into the different buckets that their mental clutter can be organized into.

We know that the way to eat the elephant is one bite at a time, so once you start seeing what the different buckets might be and how they relate to each other, these become the starting point for your process and will inform your way forward.

When I started working with Gloria, she had a big career decision to make and didn't know what to do. She felt stuck. She was caught in a swirl of thoughts and kept going around in circles, always landing on the same question of should I do A or B? Every exploratory question I asked resulted in us going around the same circles over and over again, circles that expanded each time new thoughts came up, feeding into her existing pattern.

Going through this survey step changed everything for her. Together, we simply put on paper everything that was floating in her mind: the pros and cons of each option, her worries, her fears, her ambitions, her family situation and responsibilities, her desires. Once these were all out of her head, she realized that the decision did not need to be made for another year. She identified steps she could take that would give her further data, helping to inform her future choice in both a factual and an emotional way.

Together, we listed the different buckets her thoughts belonged in, put time frames around critical decision points, and focused on each piece one after another. This took away the panic and meant she could think clearly again, focusing on one step at a time. The key was to stop the whirlwind of brain activity and separate out, then organize, the various strands of thinking.

I now want to take you on a tour of the different areas of mind clutter that you might be carrying and could form some elements of your survey, the starting point of your mental decluttering process.

Taking a tour of mind clutter
Work

Your job will probably take up a large part of your thinking much of the time, simply because of how much time you are physically working compared to other activities. I have already covered a few areas to do with noticing the clutter in your physical workspace and environment (see Chapter 4). The performance of your job will also take up much of your brain space.

How much mental clutter does your work create for you? How many projects are you dealing with, how many emails land in your inbox, how laborious are the various processes that you need to follow to get basic things done? One of the challenges I find my clients are often faced with is that they spend most of their time and headspace dealing with firefighting and sitting in meetings, and that there is not much resource left for the deeper thinking – the strategic thinking that requires a clear mind. This is one of the topics that I cover in speaking engagements and I always see the audience nodding in agreement when I mention our distractibility and lack of focus on the big and meaningful stuff.

In addition to all these work pressures, what clutter are you generating for yourself around your work? How much of your headspace is taken up by judging yourself, telling yourself stories about why you don't belong in that room or why you shouldn't apply for that next promotion, even though you watch others around you move up the career ladder while you stay put?

It's easy to spend huge amounts of mental energy on things that are not helpful, not useful or don't move you or your projects further on. Start applying a ranking system around what you are thinking about and notice when you are spending too much time on thoughts that don't bring you any value.

Household

Unless we employ staff, most of us will spend a fair amount of our brain processing power on thinking about, organizing and running our household. It's not a glamorous activity. It's not something we would regularly feel a great deal of satisfaction about. We see it more as a chore than anything else, but nevertheless it is relentless in its demands. There is the cleaning, the maintenance, the food shopping and cooking, the paperwork, the happiness levels of others in our household, the pets… the list goes on. And crucially, we are never done with it all. It is not something we can complete, tick off and put away. It is ongoing, always there.

Running a household can take up not only a significant amount of your energy and time but also a good amount of your headspace. It is an area that is often left out of your field of vision and awareness when considering what you have on your plate, even if it is in your thoughts a lot. When you think of your capacity, whether of time or energy, running the household does not feature as a competing activity. It's just something you do alongside everything else.

Earlier, I joked about having staff. How much of your headspace would be freed up if you didn't have to think about the laundry, the car service, or what you will have for dinner? I am not suggesting that we all hire armies of butlers, but rather that we see this stuff for what it is: work that requires our attention. This also ties in with the 'digital housework' and 'shadow work' described in Chapter 6.

When you survey your mental landscape, notice that a portion is consumed by your household. It's normal, it's the same for everyone – so acknowledge that running your home takes time and energy and allocate some capacity to it. And if you have someone in your household who looks after many of the household tasks so that you don't have to, know and acknowledge how much of their headspace and energy it requires.

Finances

Whether we talk much about it or not, money plays a huge part in our lives. We spend a lot of time thinking about it and it drives many of our decisions, so I want to touch on a few points here around the mental clutter it can generate for us.

How much are you worth?

There is something slightly uncomfortable in talking about money. At least, there is in the UK, although in some other cultures people will be happy to openly discuss what they earn (or want people to think they earn!), how much they have in their bank account, and how much others earn. Wealth has always been hugely important to civilizations, with ways of showing it either openly or more subtly to signal where we fit into society.

What you own and how much you earn can be a powerful determinant in how you feel about yourself and others. Whether you are trying to keep up with your friends by purchasing the latest luxury car model or struggling to make ends meet and put food on the table, money plays a huge part in this thinking. Worrying about money can take up a significant amount of your headspace, creating so much mental clutter that it can cloud all other thoughts. Financial worries are so widespread that the National Health Service in the UK even has a page dedicated to the topic in its mental health section (NHS 2023).

I often work with clients who find themselves in a place where they feel stuck. They are in a highly stressful job that doesn't fulfill them, or in a relationship with someone they don't want to be with, or in a house or town they don't like, all because they think they have no other choice. They are dependent on the salary, the financial support, or the affordability of a postcode. Money and the perceived limit of options keep them in a place that makes them unhappy. It makes them feel that control over their lives has slipped away from them. Is that something you recognize?

Our relationship with money is complex. It is a product of how we grew up, what has happened to us in our life, how we feel about ourselves, the culture we live in. And that complexity translates into a personal pattern of mental load while you're thinking about it. What is your relationship with money? What are your beliefs around your worth, money and what makes you rich? How much of your headspace is taken up by thinking about money?

Where mental and physical clutter collides
A different aspect to our finances is the practical side of managing our money. In today's world, it is increasingly complicated to understand all the small print that needs signing simply to open a bank account. Almost everyone has one or several credit cards and maybe several bank accounts. We are encouraged

to shop around for the best interest rate, the best deal on new bank accounts, or 0 percent interest credit card transfers. In the UK, there is even a quick and simple standard online process to switch current accounts to support this endless flux. In addition, there are pension investments to think about, and the number of financial products available is simply mind-boggling.

All of this needs constant attention and effort for you to keep on top of things. Managing these different accounts and cards involves paperwork (or electronic communication) that needs filing. It creates mental clutter and, depending on your personal circumstances, can be hugely stressful. As with anything, hiding it all away into a dark metaphoric or real-life drawer might be tempting, but it will not make it go away.

It might feel as if this type of financial clutter belongs in the physical clutter section, and it partly does. But I feel that it also sits in the mental clutter bucket because of how it plays on our minds and can affect us in so many ways.

I once worked with a client who brought me in to help her sort out her office. Francis had been running her own business for a few years and found that it was not as successful as she wanted it to be. She felt she had hit a wall and didn't know how to move forward. When I asked her about the papers that were piled all over her desk and office floor, she sighed and said she didn't know what was where, but it was a mixture of invoices, client notes and business documents, as well as craft supplies for when she had the time to spend on her hobby.

We started going through her papers and sorting them into piles, all the while talking about her business. It transpired that she enjoyed her work with her clients but found all the administrative tasks around invoicing and budgeting daunting and difficult. She put aside anything to do with her finances and didn't pay any attention to them. Over time, the paperwork piles grew and attracted other papers and letters, until she had let it all get on top of her and she felt that the whole business had slipped out of her control.

She put a filing system in place, simplified her finances and hired someone to help with invoicing her clients. The result was that by removing the stress and mental clutter caused by her aversion to all things financial, Francis had created some headspace and found renewed energy to focus on growing her business again. Six months later, her business was thriving.

It's useful to recognize how much of your headspace is taken up by thinking about money. How much stress do you experience from looking after your finances? How could you simplify things? Do you have any unused memberships that can be canceled? Can any unnecessary bank accounts be closed?

Looking after our health

Our health and the associated topics of exercise and diet, essentially everything to do with wellbeing, can take up a huge amount of thinking space. Whether it is all the internal chatter around what you think you *should* be doing or not doing, the ways you might be judging yourself, or the time you spend researching or organizing tasks related to your health, this is an area that can create a huge amount of head clutter.

This is also likely to be a topic and thinking pattern that has been with you for a while, so it will be familiar to you. Or perhaps something has recently changed in your life around your health that you have to deal with and adapt to, and that is taking up headspace. It can be easy to take our bodies for granted, until something stops working as it used to.

Staying healthy is an ongoing, daily consideration linked among other things to your food, sleep and exercise habits. If it is something that you are finding tricky or difficult, it can create not only an inordinate amount of mental noise, but likely also a fair amount of emotional clutter. What is your situation around health and wellbeing? How much headspace is taken up thinking about what you eat, what you don't eat, the exercise you're currently doing, or what you're not doing and think you should?

Hobbies and activities

Another recurring theme that comes up with my clients is that they are so busy with their work, home and family that they rarely take any time for themselves, let alone for an activity as frivolous as a hobby. Hobbies are often seen as nice-to-haves, but not always realistic in terms of fitting them into their schedules. Hobbies are seen as indulgent, and when the stress increases, they are one of the first activities to be given up.

A big turning point for me was when I attended a training course that distinguished between time and energy levels. We often feel as if we don't have enough time to do things, but a more relevant dimension is our energy level for any given activity. We know that when we consider doing something we love, we suddenly feel energized, even if we felt exhausted a moment before. And that is what hobbies are for. They are a way for your brain to take a break and focus on something different for a while. Depending on your activity, it could also utilize a completely different part of your brain. It is a great way to re-energize your mind, along with any other benefits your chosen hobby might bring, such as physical health, mental wellbeing through socializing, or creative thinking.

So, figure out how you can make space for hobbies not only in your schedule but also in your mental landscape. They might in fact serve a purpose rather than being an indulgence!

Relationships and social life

Whether they are family or friends, colleagues or acquaintances, the people we are surrounded by are a part of our landscape. I will talk more about this in Chapter 10, but they are worth mentioning here for the headspace and energy that they take up.

These people will all have different influences on you: your colleagues can create an energizing work environment or make you feel inadequate; your children might bring you joy as well as worry; your partner can be supportive or a source of stress; your friends might be uplifting or drag you down; and your neighbor might be tedious or a blessing because they water your garden while you are away. We are all surrounded by our own constellation of characters. This constellation will also vary over time, when one friend or parent suddenly needs more attention and looking after due to something happening in their life.

It is easy to consider your social circle only in terms of the time and energy those people require from you, another thing that you need to fit into your busy schedule. Try allocating some of your brain processing power to the people in your life with whom you want to engage in a more meaningful way, or with whom you might simply want to spend more time because they nourish you. You might find that these interactions then become an energy boost rather than a time drain.

Other people's stuff

Some of the wonderful traits of human beings are empathy and a sense of wanting to help others and wishing the best for them. If you are not careful though, you can easily take on the worries of those for whom you care, taking on a whole chunk of mental clutter for something that is not yours to hold. And not only is it not yours to hold, but you carrying it doesn't make it any lighter for them.

Similarly, when you are in an interaction with someone and they become upset, it is likely to be their internal mental and emotional landscape that interprets the situation in this difficult way for them, rather than your actions being the main cause of their reaction. It is easy then for you to take this into your load and carry it for them, worrying about what you might have done wrong.

I am not suggesting that we never do anything wrong or hurtful. I would like to think that most of our actions and words come from a place of meaning well for others, and even if this is a bit clumsy at times, the intention is a positive one. So, with this as a baseline, if your actions or words are misinterpreted or misunderstood, it is likely that you hit a nerve you didn't know was there. And this is their stuff, not yours.

In that same vein, when you feel hurt or upset, you could pause and reflect on how your internal clutter might be amplifying the situation, or whether you are making some assumptions that are causing you to feel this way but are not necessarily the reality. The drama triangle described in Chapter 3 can also introduce a different view and help you step out of the drama of a situation.

Internal chatter, beliefs and memories

Alongside identifying what is coming from other people, paying attention to your own internal clutter will help you see the bigger picture. 'We do not see things as they are – we see them as we are' is an anonymous but useful quote. We perceive the world through our own personal views and framework of experiences. These are all completely personal to us and wonderfully diverse in their nature!

These views and frameworks are also coupled with our unique individual set of assumptions, beliefs, values, fears and biases. When we think that a situation is a certain way, then we will have made it that way for ourselves. And this is probably our biggest blind spot!

Sometimes all our internal clutter can get in our way and contribute significantly to the tangled-ness of our mind.

Paying attention and asking yourself what your assumptions might be about a particular situation, or what you might be believing in that moment, or what you are frightened of, can help unlock useful data. You might not always be able to see this for yourself, and when that is the case, you can enlist the help of a trusted thinking partner. You don't always have to do everything on your own.

Another aspect of internal clutter that I want to mention here is our memories. Alongside our thoughts and inner dialog, these can constitute a fair amount of the mental clutter that we hold. But a word of caution! Similarly to the personal framework through which we see the world, our memories are also a construct of our mind, and they are altered and edited every time we access them (Schiller et al 2010). That is not to say that all our memories are false and don't represent reality, but rather that they should be viewed with a healthy dose of curiosity. As neuroscientist Daniela Schiller said, '[M]emory is what you are now. Not in pictures, not in recordings. Your memory is who you are now' (Hall 2013).

It can be a fun exercise to recall an event with someone else who was also present and compare your memories. The best illustration I have come across around this was shared by the neurologist Oliver Sacks (2017). Through a conversation with his older brother, he realized that an event he thought he had experienced as a child and had vivid memories of was in fact not a memory of his, as he wasn't even present at the time. Other people's storytelling imprinted this event into his mind and made it as real to him as any other that he had witnessed! This is why eyewitnesses can't always be relied on to provide evidence in police investigations (Mojtahedi 2017).

Memories, especially painful ones, sometimes get put aside or buried so we can get on with life. The difficulty is when they reappear and trip you up or perhaps drive a behavior or habits that you want to shed at some point. Bringing them into your awareness and lightening their load could be something that you might choose to embark on when you feel the time is right. They don't have to weigh you down forever.

Biases

A bias is a 'mental tendency or inclination, esp. an irrational preference or prejudice' (Collins 2025). In whatever we do, think or feel, we are constantly influenced by biases that affect our view of the world, of others and of ourselves. And there are hundreds of them! In this survey step, we might want to raise our awareness of the effect that biases might have on our mental landscape. Is your thinking a true representation or has it been somewhat influenced by one or several of your subconscious processes and shortcuts?

Biases are a bit like thought generators. They take in the circumstances around us and then apply shortcuts to create thoughts about the situation. I want to mention two biases in particular to illustrate this point, though there are plenty more!

First, we humans have a stronger tendency or bias to attend to negative rather than positive stimuli (Veepara et al 2020). This comes from the days when our survival depended on identifying threats quickly and is still perceptible in our behaviors today. When faced with a situation, our brains will tend to look for ways in which we are falling short, or circumstances that are not as good as we would like them to be, or that others are against us – rather than all the things that are going great. It is also why we tend to focus on all the things we haven't done yet, rather than celebrating all the small things we have done. Is this something you recognize?

The second one I want to mention here is our natural bias to perceive and retrieve mood-congruent information most easily (Becker & Leinenger 2011). This means that we will look for justification and reinforcement in our environment for what we are already thinking. This is useful to pay attention to, as you might want to look beyond the immediate data surrounding a stimulus and resulting thoughts, to examine what you might have been missing that could influence how you interpret a situation and think about it.

There are many more cognitive biases that influence our thinking without us noticing it (Kahneman 2012). When you are surveying your thoughts and mental clutter, you might like to take a step back and consider the bigger picture, asking yourself how your beliefs or biases might be interfering with your view of a situation, and how you could see things differently.

Your turn: surveying your own mental clutter

After considering these different areas of mental clutter and adding any others that you are currently carrying that weren't specifically touched on, it is time to put pen to paper (or stylus to screen) and map out your mental landscape.

What are all the thoughts that you are carrying at the moment? If they've been swirling around in your mind for a while, some thoughts might be familiar, and others might be niggles that aren't yet fully formed ideas. Get all of them out of your head and onto a sheet of paper or a screen in front of you.

1. Take ten minutes to sit still and write down every thought that comes into your mind. Your mind will wander or maybe stay stuck in a loop in one place. That's

completely fine. When you notice that happening, bring it back to simply listing your thoughts.

2. What challenges and pressures do you currently feel, and what mental clutter do these generate for you?
3. Which thoughts keep you awake at night? What worries you?
4. Capture any reflections from the previous chapters, in particular Chapter 6 around your digital life and footprint.
5. Download all your thoughts into a brain dump so that you can see everything visually, using any format that works well for you: a list, a mind map, a drawing. This exercise alone can be hugely cathartic.

Here is an example of what your mental survey output might look like:

Thoughts
I'm worried that my project isn't going to schedule.
In order to be well viewed at work, I need to work long hours, attend every meeting and respond to every email that I receive.
My partner doesn't listen to me properly anymore and that makes me feel lonely.
I should exercise more and eat more healthily.
I'm constantly distracted and interrupted by messages and notifications.
I'm ashamed of the state of my house. I should really sort it out and tidy things.
I need to get my head around my pension situation.
...

Step 2: Plan

Once you have a picture of what you are carrying in your mind and you can see the mental clutter in a more tangible form, you have the starting point for your decluttering process. The second step in the method is to determine what you want your mental landscape to look like and plan how you will create that.

Do you want a Zen-like mind all the time? Some of the time? Is your brain running at full speed every waking hour and you simply want to slow it down every now and again? Which of these thoughts represent situations that you want to address/resolve/fix?

Often, when we carry a heavy mental load, the likelihood is that a large proportion of thoughts will be negative in some way. They are worries, dissatisfactions and fears because these are the ones that we tend to dwell on rather than the good stuff. Remembering all the benefits of positivity from Chapter 2, do you want to choicefully bring more positive thoughts to your attention? Ruminating on and carrying negative thoughts is a downward-moving spiral, reducing your headspace for other things and generally making you feel bad.

Notice your language and how you describe your thoughts. If they are negative thoughts, it can feel as if they have control over you, that you have little or no power to change things and make them better. Reframing your thoughts and focusing on the positive shifts you from a place of overwhelm to one where there are things you can do. You are in control again.

1. Look at the download of thoughts that you created and consider what you would like to do with each one. Some of these thoughts will translate into easily identifiable tasks that can be planned and scheduled, and others might require a bit more thinking around them.

2. Identify what clutter you want to filter and keep out of your mental landscape by setting up some boundaries, perhaps for a while, to protect your time, focus and attention.

3. Use your wonderful creativity and resourcefulness to think of all the possible actions that you can take to move away from worry and toward calm. Capture them with a timeline according to your priorities or any other factors that might be relevant.

4. You might find that as you work through your different items, some of them aren't ones you want to do anything about right now. Feel free to either park actions for later or maybe decide you don't want to do them at all. Making that decision can help remove the mental load for it if you decide to put it aside for a specific time frame. Do feel free to be generous with the 'don't do' items!

5. Experiment with and adopt some habits to clear your mind when you want some quiet time. There are evidence-based techniques that can help with this:

   - Journaling (Baikie & Wilhelm 2005): Take a break and simply survey your mental landscape or do some stream of consciousness writing whereby you put pen to paper and record what passes through your mind.
   - Mindfulness (Grossman et al 2004): Sit comfortably, close your eyes and focus on your breath for a few minutes. It's normal for your mind to wander. When that happens, simply bring your attention back to your breath.
   - Exercise (Harvard Medical School 2020): Find any form of exercise you enjoy and create a habit around building it into your routine.

Continuing with our previous example from Step 1, here is what your plan might look like. I have suggested some actions, but you will know best what might work for you or what you would like to try.

Thoughts	Action	Do by	Done
I'm worried that my project isn't going to schedule.	Speak with X to understand the facts and work out how to get back on track.	Monday	✓
In order to be well viewed at work, I need to work long hours, attend every meeting and respond to every email that I receive.	Recognize that these are simply my beliefs and that I can choose to believe something different.		
	Find a friend/coach/mentor to work with to create some new beliefs.		
My partner doesn't listen to me properly anymore and that makes me feel lonely.	Plan some time out to have a meaningful conversation with my partner about what is bothering me right now.		
I should exercise more and eat more healthily.	I want to feel better and know that walking more/drinking more water/... will help me with this, so will schedule these habits with reminders.		
	Identify and select an accountability partner to help keep me motivated and on track.		

I'm constantly distracted and interrupted by messages and notifications.	Switch off all notifications from all platforms.		
	Set do not disturb status when doing deep thinking work.		
I'm ashamed of the state of my house. I should really sort it out and tidy things.	I will find someone to help me understand why this is difficult for me and get my house organized.		
I need to get my head around my pension situation.	Talk to trusted friends/ family and get recom- mendations for a financial advisor to understand the facts.		
...			

You'll notice that in my examples, many of the actions involve finding others to help with various things. You don't have to be an expert at every single task and you don't have to do everything on your own. Your habits will be easier to spot and unpick if you have a thinking partner to help notice what you're unaware of in your behaviors and thinking patterns.

Step 3: Act

The third step in the decluttering method is to bring these actions to life. Some of them will be easier to do than others. Some will be quick, and others might require a certain time period to complete. The completion dates identified will inform the order in which to tackle these.

Depending on what they are, working through these actions can perhaps feel overwhelming in itself. The idea is, of course, to ultimately create mental space and not add to the mental clutter!

Below are a few things that I learned along the way from working with many different clients.

1. Focusing on one thing at a time will get you there faster. It simplifies what your mind needs to work on, creating the mental space for good quality thinking and processing.
2. Once you start giving something your undivided attention, you sometimes realize that this thing is not that important anymore and can easily be set aside.
3. Choosing how you want to use your brain processing power naturally makes you notice your habits and behaviors more, which in itself can make it easier to make a shift.
4. Some simple techniques, from taking a break in fresh air, meditating for a moment, practicing mindfulness or taking a few deep breaths, can be immensely restorative and effective in breaking the thought swirl. Relaxing music can also have a soothing and de-stressing effect.
5. Hone your filters and boundaries to actively reduce the data overload.
6. Develop your 'saying no gracefully' muscle.

Step 4: Celebrate

Decluttering your mind can feel like a never-ending endeavor or an impossible to achieve end state because of the constant flux of your thoughts. This can make it difficult to acknowledge any progress that could warrant a celebration!

Do pay attention to the moments when you might have had a success, though, however big or small – for example, 'felt comfortable with a new project timeline', 'embraced a new technology' – and ensure that you celebrate this in a way that will feel joyful.

When I lost my running partner a few years back, I knew that my motivation would decline and I would easily find excuses to skip this regular and slightly painful exercise. Of course, intellectually I knew all the benefits of running two or three times a week. Yes, I felt better for it: I had more energy, it gave me a space to think freely without interruptions. But still, it felt incredibly hard to make myself go out and do it when it was gray and damp outside. I decided that for every ten runs I did on my own, I would treat myself to a massage. This felt like a reward that was accessible, but not so easy to attain that it was too indulgent and I didn't need to make an effort to reach it. It was a reward that worked well for me, and it kept me going until I found a new running partner.

An additional benefit of introducing a reward like this was that it made the running something positive that I was happy to do. It became a way to earn a treat rather than an obligation that I didn't want to stick to. I know, all the health benefits should have been enough but they weren't! Framing the activity into something positive made a big difference in how I approached doing it.

And now, when my new running partner isn't available, I enjoy running on my own and simply letting my mind wander. I have a routine that feels habitual and I just get on with it. The more often you do something, the more a habit is formed (Clear 2018), and I can see that in action with my running, as well as a few other things. The activity becomes less unfamiliar and out of the ordinary, all little cues that might get in the way of doing them.

1. Reflect on what would be a good reward system for you. Think about what would make it worth your while to stick with the work when it gets hard. Capture your ideas to refer back to when needed.

2. Make the time to celebrate with whatever reward you picked for yourself and fully enjoy it.
3. Celebrate each completed task!

Step 5: Evaluate

Now is the time to review what you learned from these steps so that you can make any adjustments needed to make them smoother for the next time. This is a crucial step that will provide you with the data and insights for growth and improvement.

We are often busy carrying on with our lives and don't take the time to reflect. When you are in the process of creating something new, learning and embedding unfamiliar and novel patterns and behaviors, taking the time to reflect on these will be invaluable to broaden the learning and make it that much more impactful.

1. Notice how you successfully completed one of your tasks.
2. What was different for you from your usual behavior or typical pattern?
3. Consider what enabled you to achieve this. What can you tap into next time you are facing a similar circumstance?
4. Expanding the learning, how could you use this insight or behavior and replicate the success in other areas?

This concludes Part 2, which considered your mental clutter and focused on creating mental space. When you look at your physical stuff, it is easy to see what is in your way and the tangible nature of the items makes them visible. Thoughts are not as easy to quantify and distinguish and can therefore be trickier to organize.

As you have seen, headspace and brain processing power are finite, so it is essential to consider them as such and be more mindful of what you are accumulating without noticing it. In the realm of physical clutter, when a bookshelf is full, there is no space for a new book. And so it is for your mental space too. While you are cluttered with thoughts, there is no space for anything new that you might like to introduce, or any creativity to handle a sticky situation.

In this attention economy, it is crucial that you fiercely protect your mental power and focus in order to retain your agency over how you want to utilize your valuable brain capacity, or else you simply live to get through the day. If you want to shift the dial on something, you need to create the mental space necessary to enable you to do that.

You will probably have noticed that some of your thinking is not purely analytical, a cold and clinical look at a clearly defined and organized thought process, but loaded with feelings of some sort. Our minds will also play many tricks on us to keep us in place. What makes things a bit more complicated is that sometimes we are not only talking about our thoughts, but we are at an intersection between our thoughts and how we feel. So, in the third part of the model, let's look at our emotional clutter.

Chapter summary

▶ The world is speeding up and the complexities of our lives are increasing exponentially, generating an unmanageable amount of mental clutter.

▶ Step 1: Survey your mental clutter by listing out everything that is swirling around in your mind, which will give you a visual representation of what you are dealing with.

▶ Step 2: Plan what you want your brain activity to be like. Some thoughts will require actions; other situations of mental overload require strategies for quiet time.

▶ Step 3: Act on your plan and put in place routines to look after your brain.

▶ Step 4: Celebrate every thought you put on hold, every moment you calmed your mind, every activity you executed from your plan.

▶ Step 5: Evaluate your learnings through reflection questions around new habits you are experimenting with.

Part 3

Creating emotional space

9

Understanding emotions better

After spending 16 years in the corporate world, I trained as a coach and set up my coaching practice, Creating Space. I knew that I wanted to combine my new skills with my interest in organizing physical spaces, and with my belief that we need to be mindful of what we carry in our headspace. This load might be invisible, but its weight can be as heavy as the excessive physical stuff. As I built up my business and my decluttering model, I realized that there was a missing element that had even more bearing on how we live: our emotions.

For a long time, I was out of touch with my emotions and didn't feel I wanted to open this seemingly scary box. I didn't know what to look for or what to expect, and I held the belief that 'strong = good'. And 'strong' implied not showing emotions.

I remember one particularly difficult project at work. I had been handed the responsibility of delivering a piece of work and felt proud of the trust I had been shown by being given this task. The project grew and my resources diminished as people left without being replaced. I gradually reached a point where I felt so out of my depth that I sought out a mentor for support. I spent our entire first meeting in tears. This was clearly a sign that something was badly wrong: I never cried at work! It took me many years to fully grasp what that had been about and I have learned that emotions, rather than needing to be feared, are instead an invaluable source of information about ourselves and others and have much to teach us. Had I paid attention to how I felt earlier in the project, I could have taken corrective action way before reaching breaking point.

The journey of uncovering and understanding my emotions continues, likely as a lifelong project, and I am increasingly finding that this is where I do the most impactful work with my clients. Many leaders with whom I work shut themselves off from their emotions, believing as I did that they need to remain hidden. There is a cultural aspect here too. In the UK, for example, a 'stiff upper lip' is seen as desirable, with displays of emotions avoided at all costs. In Mediterranean countries, people are often more expressive with their feelings, though how much of that is for show and how much is truly felt isn't always clear.

In any case, whatever your habits around expressing them, your emotions are key to understanding yourself. As you go through life, you collect not only things but also experiences, relationships, memories and emotions. This emotional clutter and the framework you have built to process your world is what makes you who you are today. It determines the ways in which you respond to situations and interact with people, and it also helps to explain why certain situations or people bring up specific emotions in you.

An interesting myth around emotions is that women are more emotional than men. However, when asked to monitor and record the emotions they were feeling throughout the day, men and women reported the same amount of emotion in everyday life (Feldman Barrett 2018). On average, the intensity of the emotions felt is also the same across genders. Differences start to appear in the expression of these emotions, with men generally being less forthcoming or skilled in discussing or addressing them than women (Wright 2023).

Let's delve into emotional clutter and get to know it better. To do this, we'll start by looking at what emotions are, how they can get in your way and where they come from.

Our emotional stuff

These days, we hear a lot about EQ (emotional quotient) and EI (emotional intelligence). The concept of emotional intelligence has sprung up alongside the more traditional IQ (intelligence quotient) measure of intelligence, which was increasingly seen to be lacking in providing a rounded picture of human intelligence as well as economic success.

Salovey and Mayer (1990), university professors who coined the term emotional intelligence, define it as, 'The ability to monitor one's own and others' feelings and emotions, to discriminate among them, and to use this information to guide one's thinking and action.'

Understanding your emotions and using them well will help you work better, understand others better, communicate better, resolve conflict, build stronger relationships… and the list goes on!

You experience emotions all the time. Your emotions are rooted in the complex web of your inner world, your experiences, and information from the outside world picked up by all your senses. In turn, they also provide information about you. They work alongside your brain to keep you safe and look after you, or at least they did at some point in your life.

This brings in the interesting component of time. If your emotions come from your deepest core, they have been forming over the duration of your life and were learned within a particular set of circumstances. Often, when your circumstances change, your emotional responses fail to adjust and that is when you might find yourself out of sync with your current world. How often have you told yourself to 'grow up' when dealing with a certain situation?

The reason why I have become interested in emotional clutter is because, in the same way that physical and mental clutter can get in our way, so can emotional clutter – ours and that of others. And as for physical and mental clutter, I want to emphasize that emotional clutter isn't bad. On the contrary – our emotions are a huge part of our identity, and they hold vast amounts of data about us. They can help you understand who you are, what matters to you, why you get in your own way. And they also help you understand others at a deeper level too.

Your emotions are fine-tuned radars for all sorts of information, and you ignore them at your peril. Decluttering your emotions is not about getting rid of them, or suppressing them, or even labeling them as bad. Decluttering your emotions is about understanding them better and where they get in your way, calibrating or regulating them to become a helpful tool instead.

According to Professor Ilona Boniwell and psychologist Aneta D Tunariu (2019), ignoring your emotions is generally counterproductive. 'Emotions are best attended to rather than minimized or ignored, not least since they are likely to find an outlet anyway, leaking their message and purpose into our conscious or unconscious levels of existence in spite of being neglected, concealed or denied.'

If you ignore emotions, they will manifest anyway and drive your behavior, particularly when you are stressed or tired. A far better approach is to embrace them for what they are, acknowledge them, and then use them to increase your self-awareness. What are your current thoughts about your emotional clutter? Do you see it as a valuable resource or a burden, or are you completely neutral and have no particular tendency one way or another?

When emotions get in your way

Steve contacted me at a time when he was about to start a new job. He was excited by this new opportunity; this job was a great step forward in his career and he was looking forward to the challenge. At the same time, he was trying to process how his previous job had ended. Things hadn't gone quite according to plan. The organization turned out to have a significantly different culture to the one he had encountered during the hiring process, his role had not been what he had expected, and he ended up spending all his time wrapped up in company politics rather than getting the job done. His frustration grew, alongside feelings of guilt around not doing the work he was paid to do, as well as anger about how the company operated.

Now it was time to put these emotions to rest. Steve wanted to start the new job afresh, as well as reconnect with his sense of enthusiasm and energy for his career. He did not want the negative feelings from the old job to taint and spill into the new one. We worked through what he was feeling, how he might handle a similar situation in the future, and how he could leave the emotions behind while holding on to the learnings from the experience. He cleared his decks to have the emotional space to fully engage in a positive and confident way with the new job, his new colleagues, and a new set of team and company dynamics.

Emotions are incredibly powerful forces. Whether you are dealing with a situation or a relationship, either with someone else or with yourself, emotions play a big part in how you behave and what you choose to do. Often, their role is to keep you right where you are, because that is the familiar place and it feels safe.

Change can be difficult to make happen, and the bigger the departure from where you are now, the stronger the resistance will be. Organizations are confronted with this all the time. Unless they invest resources in managing change, their employees will feel all manner of negative emotions while they try to come to grips with the uncertainty of what will happen to them and what the new state will be. Countless hours are wasted on worrying and speculating about what might be if the process of change is not handled well.

It is the same for us with any change that we might want to introduce for ourselves. There will be internal resistance as we try to shift away from the usual and move toward the new, and creating some emotional space will allow this to happen more smoothly. Is this something that you recognize in yourself as well? How are your emotions getting in the way of your ambitions and desires at the moment? Are anyone else's emotions getting in your way? What would you do if you could set aside the forces of your emotions for a while?

What are emotions?

You probably have a sense of a definition, but I want to spend a bit of time delving into the terminology to set the scene. The Oxford Languages Dictionary (2025) defines emotion as 'a strong feeling deriving from one's circumstances, mood, or relationships with others.' To unpick this and take it a step further, consider the essential features of an emotion, which Oatley, Keltner and Jenkins (2006) summarize as follows:

'(a) a conscious mental state with recognizable quality of feeling and directed toward some object,

(b) a bodily perturbation of some kind,

(c) recognizable expressions of the face, tone of voice, and gesture,

(d) a readiness for certain kinds of action.'

I will expand on these different elements in turn. First, there is the 'object', a stimulus of some kind. This can be a person, or a comment, a memory, a situation. You take in all the information and data about this stimulus and assess it against your internal framework. Then, based on your past experiences or on similar historical situations, you identify how you might need to respond to stay safe. These strategies will have been developed at various stages in your past, and they are now your go-to responses and reactions because they were successful for you at some point.

Second, our response to this stimulus will elicit a combination of physical manifestations. If you are angry or upset, this might cause your heart rate to rise and your breathing to speed up and become shallower. All of these are caused by a surge in cortisol (also known as the stress hormone) in your body. On the other hand, if you are content or happy, you might feel a warmth inside you, you might skip or have a spring in your step, and your body will be flooded by serotonin, oxytocin and other feel-good hormones. Your emotions determine many aspects of your physical body and demeanor.

Third, your face and the way you express yourself change and give clues about which emotions you might be feeling. Whether you are raising your voice, smiling, or crossing your arms, you are signaling what is happening for you internally. A watch-out here is that people will not necessarily have the same facial expression to convey a specific emotion (Feldman Barrett 2018). The idea of a universal expression of emotion is a fallacy; each facial expression will depend on the individual and the context.

Finally, as I mentioned earlier, emotions will determine our actions. When you are faced with immediate danger and respond with a fight or flight mode, the link between emotion and action is obvious. In many other circumstances, it is far less so. You might think that you are making your decision based on sound, rational logic, but chances are that your emotions will have had far more to do with things than you imagine.

If you were to reflect on your awareness of your emotions, what symptoms do you experience that indicate different emotions to you? How familiar are you with noticing the link between how you feel emotionally and physically?

There has been an interesting evolution in the concept of emotions. The original theory was that emotions were a response to a stimulus, as per the description above. We were at the mercy of them, and they were something that happened to us. A line of research by neuroscientist Lisa Feldman Barrett (2021) is now considering that, rather than being simply reactive, our brain is in fact predictive and our emotions are constructed rather than being static. This is a rather exciting prospect! It means that you have agency around your emotions and how you feel. You can decide what meaning you want to give to your physiological experience. It takes the familiar concept of reframing a situation to a new level: you can reframe physical manifestations to signal a different emotion than the one based on your past experiences. A typical example here is that the palpitations and sweaty hands attributed to a fear of getting on stage and speaking to an audience can be reframed to mean feeling excited by the opportunity to present your ideas.

Where do emotions come from?

Emotions are essentially the product of different parts of your brain working together to create a feeling and come to a decision on how to act.

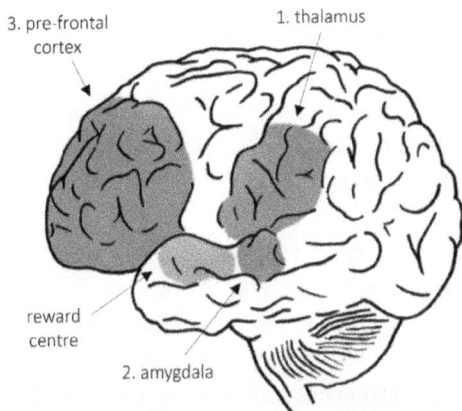

Emotions are created in three steps:

1. The thalamus processes the information from the outside world picked up by our senses.
2. The amygdala determines your emotional response to the situation based on the information from the thalamus and the level of threat in the environment.

3. The prefrontal cortex, the executive function that was introduced in Chapter 5, processes the context and regulates the responses of the amygdala.

What happens between Steps 2 and 3 is the interesting part, as the prefrontal cortex is essentially what regulates your basic, raw and instinctive response to a situation (Berboth & Morawetz 2021). The interaction between the prefrontal cortex and the amygdala determines your responsiveness to stress: the stronger the prefrontal cortex, the lower your stress levels, as it inhibits the response of the amygdala (Shapiro 2021). But when negative feelings are present, the brain responds by secreting the stress hormone cortisol, which inhibits the prefrontal cortex from effectively processing information, meaning that you will respond with a higher intensity emotion (Arnsten 2009).

Do you have a sense of what your natural tendency is when responding to situations? Do you respond from a raw emotional place or from a more reflective place? What do you notice about your prefrontal cortex intervening? Is your response different depending on the situation? What or who triggers stronger emotions for you?

When you consider your emotions, and in particular regulating them, you might tend to focus primarily on your unpleasant or negative emotions. So, what about the pleasant emotions, the ones that make you happy? Well, these engage both the nucleus accumbens and the ventral tegmental area, also known as the reward system. Not only does this reward system process the data from your senses, like the amygdala and the prefrontal cortex, but in addition, it can learn. It includes past experiences and memories before deciding on the best response, one that will be based on how well a particular decision has served you in the past. And this is the biggest asset of the reward system: its main function is all about learning. Whether it be short-term goals or long-term goals, you can identify what habits you would like to develop and teach your reward system to support you in achieving them.

So, your emotions, though they might feel out of your control and something that 'happens to you', are in fact a construct of your brain. This is not hugely surprising when you consider all the other things your brain is capable of, but nevertheless worth sitting with for a moment to consider its implications.

Chapter summary

▶ Emotions can at first appear scary and overwhelming, but getting to know them will give you valuable insights into who you are.

▶ Any change is likely to cause an emotional response, and the bigger the change, the stronger the emotion.

▶ Pay attention to how your emotions are getting in the way both in what you are currently doing and in embracing new things you might like to try.

▶ Emotions are usually triggered by a stimulus. They will elicit a combination of physical manifestations, expressions of the face, tone of voice and gesture, and then lead to an action.

▶ Your emotions are constructed rather than being static, meaning that you can reframe physical manifestations to signal a different emotion than the one based on your past experiences.

▶ A healthy prefrontal cortex will temper the intensity of your emotions (more on that in Chapter 11).

10

Starting to face your emotional clutter

One of the challenges of engaging with your emotions is that they can seem mysterious. You know that you are feeling something, but you can't necessarily explain it or describe it. This chapter is all about becoming more familiar with your emotions, introducing a framework and language for them, and looking at how conflict and positivity fit in.

Breaking it down

There are several dimensions that researchers use in their work to categorize or group emotions. The first dimension is the **intensity** of the emotion or feeling. This will range from low intensity or energy, like sadness, to high intensity, like anger or passion. The second dimension is **pleasantness**. This scale runs from unpleasant, like disgust, to pleasant, like happiness. Another dimension is whether the emotion leads you to **approach or avoid** something. From this angle, there is a notion of movement, of the drive to a particular action. Does the emotion you are feeling drive you to approach a situation (for example, joy), or does it make you avoid it, as in the case of fear?

Combining the intensity dimension with either one of the two others on a graph allows us to represent emotions and feelings in a visual way. Here is a graphic that illustrates this. I have selected to depict the dimensions of intensity and pleasantness, which is based on psychologist James A Russell's circumplex model of affect (1980). Considering the basic emotions of anger, disgust, fear, joy, sadness and surprise, they could be plotted as follows:

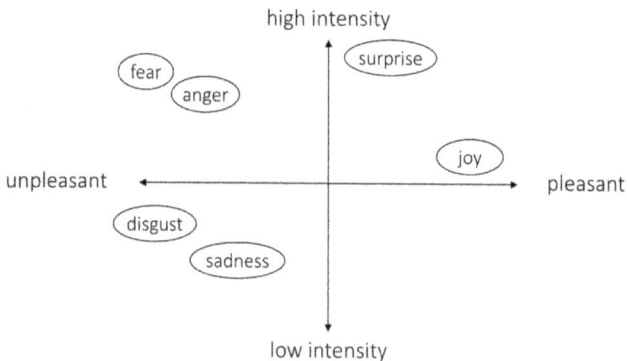

high intensity

surprise

fear

anger

joy

unpleasant ←——————————————→ pleasant

disgust

sadness

low intensity

Considering these dimensions, where do you feel that you spend most of your time? How quickly do you move from one end of a scale to another? Or are you mostly in the middle?

The broad categories of emotion are a great starting point, and using the concept of intensity allows you to refine the perception of your experience. Now let's see how you can fine-tune your awareness even more.

Learning a new language

When you think or talk about emotions, some words will be more familiar than others. The basic emotions are generally described as anger, disgust, fear, joy, sadness and surprise (or slight variations on this theme), and unless you suffer from alexithymia (the inability to identify and describe one's own emotions), you can probably recognize and label these easily.

At this point, I also want to bring up the concept of feelings. Whereas emotions are the result of physical sensations in the body and their interpretation by the amygdala (as seen in Chapter 9), feelings are what you experience consciously as a result of these emotions. They are how your mind processes these sensations and the thoughts and frameworks it applies to make sense of them. Feelings are often more complex than emotions as they could be a combination of several different emotions and your reactions to them. Scientists are interested in making a distinction between the two, but for the purpose of this book and to keep things simple, I will use the terms interchangeably.

Back to labels. When you find yourself in more complex emotional states, it can be trickier to find the words to precisely express your emotions or feelings. We know how difficult it is to try to communicate with someone in a foreign language when we either don't know how to ask a question or don't understand their answers. Trying to express your emotions when you don't have the vocabulary for it can be equally frustrating.

Patricia's story illustrates this point perfectly. When I met her, Patricia felt lost. She was working hard, had a few difficulties with colleagues who she didn't get along with and made her feel inadequate, and seemed like a rubber band ready to snap. She had come to me because she knew that something had to change, though she wasn't sure what that might be or look like.

When trying to delve into how she was feeling, we discovered that she knew only two words to describe emotions: fear and anger. As a result, this meant that whenever she wanted to express how she felt, it was one of those two words that she had available to her. Of course, she experienced happiness and joy at times, but these didn't register for her and she didn't take them in as such. Whenever she tried to look inside, she always came back to fear and anger. Expanding her vocabulary around emotions, seeing that there were other concepts and terms that she could use to describe how she felt more accurately, opened up a whole new world for her. As a result, Patricia grew in self-awareness and self-confidence. She also transformed how she related to other people, seeing them not only as a source of either fear or anger, but all manner of subtler or more positive influences too.

A fluency around the language of emotions is something that we don't necessarily grow up with, so we don't always have the awareness that something might be lacking for us to process our lived experience. In his book *Permission to Feel* (2019), Professor Marc Brackett lays out why helping children express their feelings will make them function better as adults. What you can't express remains something that you are unable to speak about, think about, explore and deal with. So the better you are able to describe and label your emotions, the better you can understand them, the more familiar they become and the easier it is to manage them. You might trip a little over the word 'label' as it might carry some negative connotations, but here I am simply using it to convey the concept of 'putting something into words'.

Remembering the dimensions that I described earlier, the intensity is a useful measure to keep in mind. For example, if you can differentiate between being mildly concerned versus panicked, you can be more refined in adjusting your behavior in this particular situation. You can diffuse your state simply by labeling it correctly. This use of scaling is helpful when you are talking about your unpleasant emotions, which is where people are usually trying to make an adjustment or a shift. But it can also be hugely insightful when you consider your pleasant emotions: when you are trying to define which life goals to pursue, would you rather choose something that makes you feel pleased, or something that makes you feel completely exhilarated?

Having a range of words to describe your emotions and feelings means that not only will you be able to get nearer to expressing precisely what you feel, but you will also gain a better insight into where they might come from (Brown 2021). Labeling your emotions is the first step to seeing them for what they are so that you can begin to work with them. I have included a sample list of words to describe emotions in Appendix 1 (available to download from my website at startcreatingspace.com/book). This is by no means an exhaustive list; it is simply a memory jog for terms that might be buried a bit deeper in your mind and could benefit from being brought to the surface. There are many more, so you might like to build your own list and keep it to hand.

As an exercise, you could journal your emotions throughout one day, using as broad a range of vocabulary as possible. Take the time to tap into what is happening inside and probe a bit more deeply than simply the six basic emotions listed at the beginning of this chapter. Notice how the accuracy of the language gives you greater insights and makes you feel different about a situation.

Conflict and our emotional clutter

We might not like it much, but conflict is inevitably a part of life. Whether we are in conflict with others, or perhaps in conflict with ourselves, every now and again we will be faced with a situation where a disagreement needs to be resolved. And when we find ourselves in such a place, our emotional clutter can get in the way and cloud our judgment.

Conflict often arises when emotions are already running high. You might be stressed, tired or feeling overwhelmed by everything that is on your plate, so when the final straw drops, you snap. You are already so cluttered with your own stuff that you simply don't have the head or heart space to consider the other person, the empathy for what they might be feeling, or the patience to listen deeply and understand their point of view. The psychiatrist Steve Peters (2012) describes this impulsive, primitive part of the brain as our 'inner chimp', which is driven purely by emotion and bypasses all logic and reflection. When you are at capacity, your inner chimp is more likely to leap out, your emotions take over and you are stuck right in the middle of the game.

You might find that certain people or situations trigger a familiar response pattern. In Chapter 3, I introduced the drama triangle as one way of understanding the different dynamics of conflict. Taking a step back in the moment or later to examine which role or roles you find yourself acting out in a particular situation (perpetrator, victim or rescuer) can give you useful information about the game at play when you are involved in a clash.

In addition, considering your emotional clutter and how it affects you in these states can be incredibly useful in finding a way to resolve your conflicts. Getting to know your own emotional landscape will enable you to identify what is happening for you in different situations, which the new words from the previous chapter can help with. You then have a choice about how to shift your habits and which new behaviors you might want to adopt.

A key step to this is sitting with your emotions and familiarizing yourself with them. They will often come from a place of self-preservation and survival, making you behave in a way that is intended to keep you safe from perceived harm, hurt, failure or embarrassment. In other cases, your emotions can be a signal that some of your core values are being violated. Understanding what your emotional clutter is protecting you from can help you see how you could behave in a more appropriate, constructive, calm and measured way. Similarly, taking the time to understand what the other party is fearful of in this conflict can help address their worries in a more useful way too.

You might even consider sharing your vulnerability in order to connect more meaningfully with others, as well as offering them the opportunity to be vulnerable. Generally, when we are feeling strong negative emotions, it is because we have a need that is not met. This need might not always be obviously recognizable, so examining your inner landscape to try to bring it to light will be immensely helpful. As a starting point, an unmet need is often a variation on the theme of wanting to be seen, heard or loved.

What patterns do you notice in your own conflicts and do you have a sense of the emotions at play? What might your emotions be trying to protect you from, and how could this information help in resolving conflicts you might be experiencing?

Our subpersonalities

Conflicts usually happen with other people, but we can also be in conflict with ourselves, and this is an area where psychosynthesis can be helpful. This is an approach to psychology developed by Roberto Assagioli (2000), which suggests that an individual is not only a product of their past experiences but also a combination of their life journey, spiritual development, psychological healing and self-realization. A key element of psychosynthesis is the idea that every one of us is a sum, a synthesis of many subpersonalities.

You might be familiar with this idea. We have common expressions that point to this concept, for example, when we say: 'A part of me wants to do this, but another part of me doesn't.' This inner tension represents different subpersonalities that have different drivers, preferences and needs. This idea that you are a sum of many parts with different needs can help bring clarity when you find yourself trying to understand your different emotions in particular contexts. It is especially useful when you catch yourself reacting in a slightly unexpected way in certain circumstances, or when you do or say something that seems out of character. In those situations, you might like to ask yourself who you were in that moment and which part of you was expressing itself.

Kyle came to me because he wanted to understand more about his emotional clutter, and specifically his fear of public speaking. He couldn't understand why he was finding this so difficult. He was a successful leader in a large manufacturing business and regularly spent his time communicating with his teams and managers. He was confident when meeting with smaller groups, but when it came to speaking on stage to a large audience, he was terrified. This made no sense to him.

When we examined his subpersonalities, and in particular the one that was fearful of public speaking, he realized that this part of him came from his school days when he was regularly made fun of by his classmates. This was the time when he developed an aversion to standing at the front of a room. In becoming more familiar with this subpersonality, he noticed that this part of him needed reassurance and protection, and also acceptance by his peers. He understood that his abilities today were different from those from his school days, and that the context was also not the same as the classroom dynamics from the time when this part of him developed. Armed with this new knowledge, his stage fright diminished hugely. He was able to apply his adult mind to his childhood emotions and temper the intensity and strength of the fear. Trepidation was still present, but it was nothing compared to the anxiety he used to have.

Having many subpersonalities is completely normal. A lot of my coaching now involves working with my clients' subpersonalities, as these provide such insightful data that can make a huge difference to their understanding of themselves. You might want to look out for yours, to discover more about where your emotions come from. The purpose of this inquiry is to get to know yourself better and to shine some light on those parts of you that you might not know so well. I have included a step-by-step exercise in Appendix 2 (also available to download from my website at startcreatingspace.com/book) to help you through examining your subpersonalities.

Dipping into positive psychology

I talk about positive psychology in Chapters 2 and 8 in the context of both our physical and mental clutter, but it is incredibly relevant to the field of emotional clutter too.

Earlier, I suggested different dimensions against which to plot emotions in order to categorize and make sense of them, and one of these was pleasantness/unpleasantness. This dimension can also be described as positive (pleasant) or negative (unpleasant). Barbara Fredrickson, one of the most prominent researchers in this field, who has been studying the effects of positivity since 1990, has found that, unsurprisingly, emotions play a huge part in her work as they are instrumental in how we operate in the world.

Her findings invariably show the tremendous benefits of positive emotions (Fredrickson 2009), and these benefits are not only short lived. For example, you feel happy in this moment and therefore enjoy a conversation with your friend more and therefore feel more connected, make healthier food choices and feel physically more alert and energized. Her 'broaden-and-build theory' also proposes that experiencing positive emotions has a longer-term effect by suggesting that they:

'- broaden our thought–action repertoires,
- undo negative emotions,
- help build resilience, and
- facilitate the kind of psychological resources that help us thrive'. (Fredrickson 2004)

Positive emotions have an array of positive side effects for creativity, thinking patterns, mindset and ability to cope with adversity, and they can also be put to use to undo the physiological damage inflicted by negative emotions. Experiencing positive emotions helps to calm the mind and the body. Having that broadened thought–action repertoire induced by positive emotions reduces the grip that the negative emotions have on the body.

Earlier, we looked at how your emotional clutter can affect your relationships and conflict in your life. Well, emotions also affect how we feel about others in general (Fredrickson 2009). When we feel positive emotions, we are more open to others, feel more connected to them, have more empathy and are more likely to understand their complexities. Positive emotions are good all round and have a huge impact on how we feel, how we operate in the world, how motivated we are to move toward our goals, how healthy we are physically, and how connected we feel to others.

But we can't be happy all the time, so what about negative emotions? We all experience them, so where do they fit in?

To produce a rounder picture, further developments in the field of positive psychology include negative emotions (Ford et al 2018). They are associated with constricting our thought and action, and continue to be seen as detrimental to our wellbeing. They are, however, now incorporated in the study of positivity simply because they are a part of the human condition. And negative emotions are not always bad; if they constrict your thought and action, they are useful when you need to focus on a particular task that requires your full attention. In those situations, you don't want to be taking in the broader picture and engaging your creativity. Maybe that's why colleagues appear a bit grumpy when they are head down in a spreadsheet!

Equally, if you experience a negative event that is high on the intensity scale, this strong and unpleasant emotion might drive you to do something about it. If you are angry enough about a particular thing, you will more likely be moved to action than if you are only mildly annoyed – the aim being an action that is legal and constructive, of course.

As with most things, the answer is in the balance, and the key is producing a picture of what that balance is for you at the moment versus where you would like it to be. Where on the scale do you spend most of your time? Do you feel generally positive or mainly negative emotions throughout the day? Do you notice a pattern? There is a theory that the optimum ratio is three positive emotions to one negative, though that specific number is somewhat debated (Diehl et al 2011). One thing is clear, though: both types of emotions are useful, and you want more positive ones than negative ones to function at your best.

Emotions in the workplace

When I am working with leaders in organizations, one of their biggest challenges is managing themselves and their teams through various emotional states. Whether you are in a job where you are managing others, or you are surrounded by people over whom you have an influence, this will be relevant to you.

Again and again, I have come across the belief that emotions don't belong in the workplace, and as per my own past experience, the idea that 'strong = good'. This might work for a while, but the problem comes when you reach points of overload, both mentally and emotionally. If you have created a climate where emotions cannot be acknowledged, this puts an additional strain on an already stretched person and it is highly likely that they are no longer as effective as they otherwise would be in their job (Fosslien & West Duffy 2019).

Emotions are data. They tell you something about others, yourself and your environment, and they are a useful source of information. If you ignore them, you miss out on a whole data set and won't be seeing the complete picture of a situation.

When negative emotions are high, it is because a need is unmet, and this is true in the workplace, too. Perhaps an employee feels as if their work is not valued, or that their contributions in meetings are ignored. Maybe they are sad to be losing a co-worker on whom they relied, or maybe they are exhausted and need a rest.

Uncovering what that unmet need is, through dialog and attentive listening, will allow you to address it and reduce the emotion. If someone in your team is cluttered by a cocktail of emotions, they are not effective or focused. You have probably had the experience of being distracted by something that has touched you deeply and that you were upset/angry/frustrated about. When you are in that state, you are certainly not focused on the work at hand or making the best decisions. I also want to reiterate that both men and women experience emotions in equal measure, so avoid making gender-based assumptions.

Emotions absolutely belong in the workplace because, until your workforce is fully replaced by robots, your employees are still people who feel all manner of things all day long. You ignore them at your peril. As a manager, it takes courage to allow emotions into the open – your own and those of others. How receptive are you to inviting emotions into the workspace? When a team member is overcome with emotion, how comfortable are you in holding that space for them? Do you allow them to safely and fully express what is troubling them without judging or trying to problem-solve immediately? How do you currently respond, and how do you want to work with emotions in the future?

Sharing how you feel is also a powerful way to strengthen a relationship of trust. There is much talk of the 'authentic leader' who brings their whole self to work. Of course, it might take some navigating to test the waters and see what you are willing to disclose, as not all of it is appropriate in every situation. But when you are able to express your feelings, you create stronger bonds with others. My invitation is to experiment with this, perhaps enrolling trusted colleagues to provide feedback while trialing new behaviors.

Finally, timing is particularly relevant when considering emotions. Have you noticed how, every time you see someone crying, they are apologizing for it, as if it is somehow a bad thing? Emotions are data, not something to be avoided. If someone is crying, they need to have the space to do so and release whatever is triggering the emotion, and that moment is not the right one to bring in logic and reasoning to solve a problem. They are not receptive at that time. Later, yes, but not in that moment. And when your own emotions are running high, it might not be the right time to express them to your team. You might choose to process them yourself first, perhaps with someone you trust, before airing them. This is where the various techniques for emotional regulation come in.

Chapter summary

▶ To get an overview of your emotional landscape, your emotions can be plotted against different dimensions such as high/low intensity and high/low pleasantness.

▶ Expanding your vocabulary around emotions and feelings will give you more breadth not only in language but also in the lived experience of the emotion.

▶ Emotions play a huge part in conflicts. High emotions are often a sign of an unmet need, so uncovering what that is will help resolve a situation more quickly and make others feel valued and heard.

▶ Positive emotions broaden and build. The more positivity you experience, the more areas of your life will grow and expand.

▶ Emotions are data, and in the workplace they are a useful source of information not to be dismissed.

▶ Sharing your own emotions when appropriate is a powerful way to build trust and strengthen your relationship with others.

11

Regulating your emotions

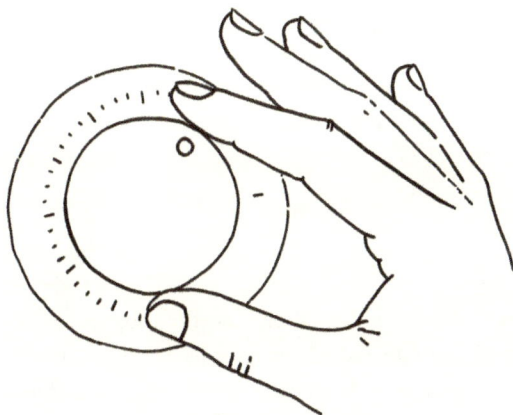

In the previous chapters, I looked at what emotions are, some language you can use to describe them, and how they might get in the way in various situations. Now let's see how to make use of all this data and utilize it to regulate your emotional responses. Because, as I mentioned earlier, your emotions don't simply happen to you. You have the power to change them.

So, what do I mean by regulating your emotions? When you regulate your emotions effectively, it means that you have some level of control over them and are able to respond to situations in a measured manner, one that feels right to you. Emotional regulation does not mean that you don't feel the emotions, or that any of them are wrong. It simply means that the actions that result from you feeling a certain way are in proportion to the stimulus that triggered them and the environment that you are in.

When we think of emotional regulation, we often consider this in the context of negative emotions. However, positive emotions might need regulating too, especially when they are high energy, like passion, for example, to stop us from taking on too much and becoming overwhelmed.

Remembering the role of the brain in this, consider the words of Lisa Feldman Barrett: 'Your brain actively constructs your emotional experiences, even those that feel out of control. If you understand the construction process, you can learn to influence it' (2017). So I will look at this construction process and how you can go about influencing it.

Change the stimulus

The first feature of emotions is the object, or stimulus. Something from the outside world is picked up by one or several of your senses and feeds into the various processes of your brain to create a system of emotions. One way of changing your emotional response to that situation is to change one or several of its parameters, or to remove yourself from it altogether.

Of course, this won't always be possible or appropriate, but in some cases, it could certainly be an option to experiment with. Avoidance might not necessarily be the best way to handle a situation in a mature manner, but it could allow you to take a step back and examine what is happening while you identify other strategies that can help you in the future.

Another aspect of this is to reframe the situation. Is that person angry with you, or have they had a difficult conversation and you happen to be the next person they speak to? We have probably all been in a situation where our emotions were running high, but then a fact changed in the story, things weren't as we thought, and our emotional state shifted almost instantly.

I remember a conversation with a friend a few months after I had moved in with my husband, where I was complaining about how much of his stuff was still unpacked and creating a messy house. Rather than engage and collude with my moaning, she asked with well-meaning curiosity: 'Can you not help him?' That stopped me in my tracks and immediately shifted my focus away from nagging and instead toward thinking creatively about how I might indeed do just that. My emotions shifted immediately from high-intensity negative to high-intensity positive. That is how effective reframing can be.

Read the label

In his research, Matthew Lieberman has found that labeling your emotions can diminish their intensity. When you label them, you are no longer at the mercy of some strong, unknown emotion that leaves you feeling powerless and cluttered. Instead, you are identifying, naming and acknowledging it, which reduces its grip on you (Lieberman & Torre 2018).

It is not always easy and straightforward to find the right label or word. Sometimes several might fit and you might be unsure of which is the right one. In that case, try them all, one after the other, and see which one feels the most representative, or perhaps a combination might be more appropriate.

This labeling allows you to remove yourself a little from the hold of the emotion by becoming its observer. This place of observation puts a distance between the heat of the situation and your reflective self, which is how you gain insight but also agency and control over how you want to respond. Look at the situation from an imagined distance, either geographical (what would this look like from ten miles away?) or temporal (what would this look like in five years' time?) to gain some perspective and remove yourself from the immediate energy of it.

Look after your brain

When I looked at where our emotions come from, I identified the different parts of the brain that were involved in creating them (Chapter 9). I shared that our prefrontal cortex effectively tempers the instinctive reactions of the amygdala, so keeping our prefrontal cortex healthy is an essential factor in helping us regulate our emotions.

In that context, one of the things to look out for is your stress levels, because when these rise, they impair the functioning of your prefrontal cortex. You probably already intuitively know that when you feel stressed, you are likely to feel less resilient and more at the mercy of your emotions.

The increasing complexities and demands of our modern, fast-paced and digital lives often mean that we live under sustained elevated stress levels, and these will have an impact on your ability to regulate your emotions effectively. Adopting strategies to reduce your stress levels will be highly effective in putting you more in control of your emotions (remember to simplify, simplify, simplify – see Chapter 7).

Use your body

Another feature of emotions is physical reaction, either in a bodily manifestation (increased heart rate) or a facial expression or gesture. One way to help you shift an emotion or reduce its intensity is to change what your body is doing. You might want to increase your activity level by going for a brisk walk or a run, adopting a power pose, or doing a few squats or other stretches, depending on your physical abilities. On the other end of the activity scale, you could try some mindful breathing, meditation or stream of consciousness writing to calm yourself down. Music has the incredible power to elicit or shift emotions instantly, so put together a playlist to listen to when you want to shift your mood and have a dance.

There are many different techniques and activities to experiment with, and you can use your creativity and imagination to find what works best for you. Smiling genuinely broadens our thought patterns, so when you're stuck for ideas, try smiling and see what comes to you then! Interestingly, doing something you enjoy is also an effective strategy for regulating negative emotions. So, have as much fun as possible when coming up with different things to try out.

Pick up a pen

Many studies have shown that journaling or expressive writing on a daily basis is highly effective and beneficial (Pennebaker 1997, Baikie & Wilhelm 2005), from the two following perspectives:

- negative emotions and processing trauma: it helps organize thoughts and emotions
- positive emotions: it replays the positive effect of the pleasantness.

There is a mysterious power in picking up a pen to write on good old-fashioned paper. Our brains make different connections when we put pen to paper, in contrast to when we speak or simply think. Stream of consciousness writing, which means simply putting on paper your thoughts and feelings as they come up without trying to understand or explain them, creates a freedom that can yield surprising results.

A different kind of more intentional writing is equally potent: you have the power to rewrite your own story. I am not suggesting inventing a new past or convincing yourself of something that feels fake. I am talking about a reframe or a shift of perspective. If you tell your stories differently, the emotions that are elicited will also be different. An altered story is also an altered interior life, which I find hugely empowering.

What's on your plate?

The link between diet and physical wellbeing is something we are able to have a conscious experience of, for example recognizing the difference between feeling energized after eating a nutritious meal versus feeling sluggish after a burger or a pizza. As different fields of science and research expand, the impact of food on mental and emotional health is providing a better understanding of how our gut also impacts our brain and mood (Appleton 2018).

There is increased focus on the longer-term impact of eating a diet containing highly processed foods, and results are showing a link between these foods and brain health (Gomes Gonçalves et al 2023, Bhave et al 2024). Ultra-processed foods are also being investigated in relation to their impact on the gut–brain axis via the gut microbiota and have been shown to cause metabolic disturbances and inflammatory responses with adverse effects on mental health (Song et al 2023).

The cookbook *Happy Food* by Swedish chef Niklas Ekstedt and medical science journalist Henrik Ennart (2018), is an example of using food as a way of tailoring how to fuel the body for mood rather than simply performance. Choosing a gut-friendly and mood-boosting diet of natural, fresh and varied foods will help you nourish your brain and prefrontal cortex, strengthening it to temper the impulses of your amygdala.

Paying attention to what you eat and using food to boost your brain power can be hugely effective in regulating your emotions.

A good night's sleep

I often talk about sleep, and that is because sleep is our superpower for so many things! Unsurprisingly, another benefit of sleep, alongside the ones already presented in this book, is that it helps you manage your emotions. Sleep time is when your prefrontal cortex cleanses its processes and resets itself for the next day (see Chapter 5), and it is also when you process difficult emotions and emotional regulation takes place (Cartwright 2012).

In our sleep-deprived society and at a time when needing rest is so often considered a weakness, I would like to argue that sleeping is in fact the single most impactful thing you can do to function better not only physically, but also mentally and even more importantly emotionally. So make time for it, embrace the power nap, create a beautiful and calm bedroom, and do whatever else you need to do to sleep more and better. And if you are unable to get as much sleep as you would like, for example because small children keep you awake or you suffer from insomnia, be kind to yourself and know that your emotional responses might be amplified by your tiredness.

In conclusion, there are a multitude of ways to regulate our emotions. We are all different and some of us will find a situation stressful while others won't. In the same way, some of these techniques might work better for you than others.

When you experiment with these techniques, or any others that you might think of, don't judge yourself if they don't 'work', and simply notice what is happening as a learning for the future. One technique might work for you one day and not another, and that is also fine. We are not machines! When that happens, simply notice it and try something else instead.

The key message is that it is in your power to take control of your emotions, and that is hugely exciting. If you find that you have a response that isn't helpful to you, you can choose a different one. No, it's not necessarily easy – and yes, it will require work. But it can be done.

Chapter summary

▶ Regulating our emotions effectively means that we have some level of control over them and we are able to respond to situations in a measured manner.

▶ Your brain actively constructs your emotional experiences, so you can learn to influence them.

▶ There are many techniques for emotional regulation. Experiment with them and discover what works well for you.

▶ The quickest way to shift an emotion is through music or reframing.

▶ You are not at the mercy of your emotions; you can have some control over them.

12

My method for creating emotional SPACE

After taking a look at what emotions are and how they might interfere with your life, it is now time to apply the five-step decluttering method from Chapter 1 to your emotional clutter.

Step 1: Survey

The first step is to survey your emotions. If you don't know what you're dealing with, you can't do much about it. This step is all about acknowledging and then getting to know your emotional landscape in more detail. Some of this will probably be fairly easy to do. You'll likely experience many emotions that are familiar to you and that you can easily identify, name or label. However, other emotions might not be so straightforward, and those might require a bit more contemplation, especially if they are a combination of several different ones. The list of emotions in Appendix 1 can help you with this exercise.

This work is for your eyes only (unless you wish to share it with someone else), and I would like to encourage you to be completely honest with yourself. Some emotions might be more difficult to acknowledge than others. You might be ashamed of them, they might bring up painful memories for you, or they might not be socially acceptable to show according to the environment that you grew up in or that you live in now. Be kind to yourself while you do this exercise.

Emotions are at the core of who you are, and if you deny or ignore them, they will have power over you and steal some of your agency. They drive overthinking as you try to make sense of things; they clutter you and get in the way of you achieving your goals or being your true self. I often describe emotions as living in a box in the corner of the room. You can see the box, you know it's there, but you might be fearful of opening it and looking inside.

The thing with this box is that when you are fully resourced and feeling well, you are able to regulate the emotions inside and keep the box closed. However, when you are tired or stressed, keeping the lid on the box might require more energy than you have and it will start leaking. You then find yourself trying to handle the emotions in addition to feeling the pressure around you, making you feel as if you are not in control of things as much as you would like. Surveying your emotions is, in effect, opening the box and looking inside, allowing your feelings to be accepted and acknowledged. Generally, the fear of looking is worse than whatever is inside the box, but it still takes courage.

Let me take you on a tour of different areas you might find in your box of emotions and might like to consider when putting together your survey.

Taking a tour of emotional clutter
Layers of emotions

I have already touched on the fact that some emotions will be easy to recognize and capture, others perhaps less so. Sometimes, you might not know what the emotions are about. You have a general feeling or sense of something, but you might struggle to put your finger on it and are even less able to give it a name, even after having studied the list of words in Appendix 1. You might have the language but still are not fully able to decode the sensation.

In those cases, you can simply start with what feels like the closest label and sit with it for a while until it either feels right or you try a different label. And you keep going or return to it some other time.

Emotions can also come in layers. You might feel one emotion, but there is a different one sitting underneath it. And when you reveal that one, there might be yet another one underneath it or several. Take your time to examine each emotion and determine if another one might be behind it, until you reach the real source of your feeling. This process can sometimes be lengthy, so feel free to take a break and return to it and continue your examination later.

The context

As I have covered in past chapters, emotions are complex things and the product of various systems of the brain and body. A number of variables can impact how you feel, and your feelings and responses to particular stimuli might also not always be the same. So when you survey your emotions, you might also want to capture some additional information related to the context of the situation:

- ◆ Who else was involved?
- ◆ What was your mood on that day?
- ◆ Was this a familiar emotion or response to this type of situation or do you feel differently at different times?
- ◆ How tired were you?
- ◆ What foods had you eaten?
- ◆ Is there anything else that feels relevant?

This will start to give you a picture of how external factors influence how you feel, providing you with useful information when it comes to developing a plan and taking action.

Physical sensations

Emotions are not only felt at an energetic level; they are often also felt somewhere in the body (Nummenmaa et al 2014). There are already many expressions in our language that convey this idea, such as 'having cold feet', 'having a twisted gut', 'feeling a tingle down my spine', and there is much for us to learn about how we feel by listening to our body.

As you survey your emotions, tap into what your body is telling you. A good way of doing this is to run a mindful body scan, simply noting without judgment what is there (Raypole 2022). You want to capture as much information as possible, so utilizing every source of data and insight is useful for this step.

We have a built-in automatic defense mechanism that will kick in as soon as we start exploring an area of discomfort. A reflex might be to shut away what is scary or unknown, to rationalize it, to explain it. Our brain does the work of protecting us and keeping us safe from this space of unease. But that is exactly where you want to go and explore. Because if you shut it away, it has power over you. So, I'll repeat it again: you want to notice and pay attention to what is there and withhold any judgment that might want to interfere.

When you tune into your body, you want to temporarily quieten your brain and listen to what you are feeling physically. Facing difficult and painful emotions is not easy, but the only way out is through engaging with the difficulty rather than ignoring or trying to sidestep it. Coming out the other side, the weight is lifted and you find a new freedom.

Are your emotions outdated?

We have already seen that emotions are constructed by the brain as a response to a stimulus, and that the brain also has the ability to learn and adapt its processes along the way by taking in new information. This brings us to an interesting consideration about when an emotion is first constructed, and how that might influence how you are feeling now. You might respond to a particular situation not with your adult experience and wisdom, but with a learned and remembered emotion from a time going far back into your past.

When you examine emotions that are more complex, layered or even elusive in terms of identifying and labeling them, this might be a sign that they originate from your more distant past and could require deeper attention, time and consideration than those that are more readily visible.

This is also something to keep in mind when you think about who you believe yourself to be. We often see ourselves in absolute statements: 'That's just how I am – I get angry at certain things', or 'I'm short-tempered. I know this about myself and I've always been this way'. These are beliefs that were formed over a long period of time and probably triggered by one or several repeated statements that were interpreted as facts and truths. But this is not necessarily the truth of who you are. If there is a desire to change, then there are many options to make that happen. And so it is with emotions.

Roles and different selves

We play many roles in our lives. We are someone's child, we might be a sibling, a friend, a parent, a more distant relation, a colleague, a boss, a customer, a provider, a carer... or any number of other characters. For each one of these roles, we take on slightly different shades, like a chameleon.

I have already explored various factors that influence our thoughts and behaviors. What I am interested in now are the slight variations of ourselves that we demonstrate when we play these different roles in our lives. Which ones are we comfortable with and happy in, and which ones might we like a bit less?

In any given situation, you show up in a certain way. This will be a product of a number of things, such as your mood in that moment, or the circumstances of this particular situation, who else is involved, what happened the last time you met them, or someone else they might remind you of. The role you play in this situation will also have an effect. It will touch on your identity and how you present yourself in this specific moment.

Some roles require different things from us, and we can be intentionally different in certain circumstances. You might present a confident and authoritative version of yourself in the boardroom, and a softer yet more impatient version when with your children. With all these varied roles you play and versions of you that you present, you might sometimes get a bit lost about who you are. Along with everything else I have covered in this book, this is all valuable information and you can choose what to do with it.

Your turn: surveying your own emotional clutter

All your emotions, including the negative ones, provide you with powerful insights into who you are and what drives you, creating a full picture of where you are right now. This survey will enable you first to bring your emotions to light, and then to consider what, if anything, you would like to change.

1. Considering all the information I have covered, make a survey of your emotional landscape.
   - Focus on your body and what its different parts are telling you.
   - Breathe deeply and slowly and invite your emotions to come up.
   - Maybe think back to things that have upset you in the past few weeks: what were your expectations and what was the outcome of the incident? Do you notice any repeating patterns?
2. Write a list of all these emotions. Include the name, the intensity, the context, where you think/feel they might come from, what role you were playing, and capture any notes that are relevant to you.
3. Experiment with noticing your emotions at different times of the day: do you see a pattern? Try sitting in different physical locations: does that make a difference to how you feel?
4. Try recording your emotions both when you are experiencing them and a bit later (a few hours or the next day). Does the temporal distance give you fewer or more insights?
5. Becoming an observer of your emotions takes you slightly out of the feeling and into a space of contemplation. You are not immersed in the box of

emotions but standing or sitting beside it and looking in.

Here is an example of what your emotional survey output might look like:

Emotion	Intensity	Context	Source	Notes
Appre-hension	high	Difficult conversation with a client.	Feel like I'm being judged and that I'm not respected for my experience.	Knot in the stomach, familiar pattern around feelings of low self-worth.
Passion	high	I often get carried away and volunteer for too many things, putting too much on my plate.	There are so many projects that I feel passionate about and I want to do them all.	I've always done this, partly to be well viewed by others, but end up feeling overwhelmed.
Loneli-ness	medium	I'm always alone now that I work from home more, and weekends are particularly bad.	I'd like to find a life partner to share things with.	I feel sad that I'm on my own and find it difficult to accept this openly.
...				

Step 2: Plan

Now that you have identified the emotions that are in your landscape, you have gathered a dataset that you can examine. Which of these emotions, if any, do you want to do something about? There is no right or wrong here; you get to decide what you have the appetite and energy to deal with right now.

You could look at these emotions from the angle of intensity:

- Are there any emotions that you would like to feel less strongly?
- Are there some that you would like to feel more intensely?
- Are there some that feel somewhat mysterious or scary, which only make appearances in particular circumstances or at specific times, and that you would like to shine a light on and understand better?
- Are there some parts of your body that feel frozen in certain situations, and which you would like to bring warmth to and feel more fully?

Perhaps the perspective of avoid versus approach can also be a helpful one through which to look at your emotional landscape: do you experience emotions that lead you to avoid situations, or do they encourage you to approach situations? And which would you prefer?

It can be useful to remember that 'what you focus on grows'. Actively choosing and deciding where to put your attention can be a powerful way to regulate your emotions and move from the negative ones (avoidance of threat) to the positive ones (approach to a reward). By reframing what you are focusing on, you can make a shift in how you feel. If your attention is on the difficulty, the problem, the 'what' that is making you feel this way, you will perpetuate the negative emotions. If you shift to the outcome that you would rather have, the solution to the problem, the 'what you want instead', you move toward more positive emotions. And a brilliant by-product of this is that your positive emotions will also 'broaden and build' (see Chapter 10) as well as increase motivation, becoming a self-fulfilling cycle.

With the information from the survey step, you can see what your emotional landscape looks like and can start formulating what you would like to see instead. It might sound simplistic and too much like a mechanical process, which can feel at odds and incompatible with the experience of lived emotions. But remember the work of Lisa Feldman Barrett: 'We are the architects of our experience.' You can create new frameworks through which to interpret your emotions, and you get to decide what you want this framework to be. Planning your approach will give you a path to guide you through this process.

1. Using the information from your survey, document your plan and how you will go about addressing the different emotions that you wish to tackle.
2. Pay attention to and notice the emotions that this process brings up for you. Does anything need to be added to your survey?
3. If it feels appropriate, is there anyone who you would like to involve in this work with you, either as a sounding board, accountability partner or simply as support?

Continuing with the previous example from Step 1, here is what your plan might look like:

Emotion	Action	Do by	Completed
Appre-hension with client	Have an open and honest conversation with client and ask what's causing them to question me all the time. What are their concerns and fears?	Next week	
	Reflect on reframing the relationship by remembering my worth and exploring how I can help this client.	Friday after-noon, slot in calen-dar	✓
	Take the time to go for a walk outside before future meetings with this client to clear my head of any other distractions.	Next week	
Passion	Get into the habit of not responding immediately but taking a moment to check if I have capacity for this new thing before committing.		
	Reflect on my need to be well viewed by others and how I can be supportive without taking on excessive work.		

Loneli-ness	Ideally, I'd like a life partner, but mainly I want to be able to do activities with others and meet new people. I'll research what groups are available near me.		
	I'll look up volunteering opportunities in my area.		
	I'll start a new habit of going out on the weekend for a coffee/walk/other and make a point of smiling and greeting everyone.		
...			

Step 3: Act

Using the plan that you have put together, as well as considering everything you have learned so far about how emotions work and how you might go about regulating them, pick where you would like to start. Depending on your circumstances, you might select a task from your plan that feels like the easiest or smallest, or you might want to begin with a task that feels the most urgent.

If you want anything to be different, you need to change something and start with your first step. This can feel scary, and it might also seem like an impossible task, but give it a try and be patient with yourself. You are effectively working to rearrange a framework that has been constructed over the duration of your life, a framework that your experiences, relationships and mental processes have built in order for you to function. In many cases, it will also have been a way to keep you safe.

The aim is not to get rid of your emotions – of course not. What I invite you to do is to remove the feeling of clutter that they cause. As a result, you will be able to engage more freely in everything you choose without the constraints that your emotions might put around you: the weight they might set on your shoulders, the tight grip they might have on your gut, or the squeeze of your heart. Decluttering your emotions will loosen the forces that stop you from living fully. So, with this in mind, it's time to make a start.

1. Carry out the tasks in your plan one after the other.
2. Look back and remind yourself of the goal that you identified in Chapter 1, your drivers for doing this in the first place.
3. You know yourself best. Listen to your intuition, tap into your past experiences, successes and difficulties, and be honest with yourself as you work through your plan.
4. Be realistic with the goals and milestones that you set yourself, and release all judgment, however strong the instinct might be to let it interfere and distract you.
5. If you need to adjust your plan as you go, do that.

Know that if you find this difficult, you are not alone. Don't hesitate to reach out to a trusted friend or family member, a professional or a helpline. A quick internet search will help you locate what and who is available in your area.

Step 4: Celebrate

This fourth step of the method is all about celebrating your successes to build up momentum and reinforce the motivation for continuing the work. Success can take any form you wish. It can simply be shifting from not wanting anything to do with your locked-up box of emotions in the corner to slowly pulling it into the middle of the room. It could be deciding to unlock the box and seeing what that feels like. Or it could be the satisfying feeling of having broken a cycle of dysfunctional conversations with someone who matters to you.

Whatever it is, notice it and celebrate it. Choose how you wish to mark the step forward: you can take a moment to capture the experience in writing, treat yourself to something you find enjoyable, do something you seldom take the time for, or share your joy with a friend/partner/family member. However you wish to celebrate your progress, do it every time you feel that you have achieved something. That something might well be an experiment that didn't work out, but the achievement is in the learning you are taking away for next time.

In Chapter 9, I mentioned a part of the brain called the reward center, which engages when we experience positive emotions, and outlined how one of the discerning features of this area is its ability to learn, constantly taking in information to make more accurate predictions and responses in the future. Celebrating your successes by allowing yourself to pause and take them in will feed your reward center and help you embed the changes and new patterns.

1. Pick a suitable reward, or set of rewards, for the different tasks that you have set yourself in your plan.
2. Break down each task as much as you need to, so that you can:
   - take bite-sized chunks of the bigger plan and
   - see the progress unfold.
3. Acknowledge your achievement or your attempt at a task that simply resulted in greater insights.
4. Take the time to enjoy yourself and fully feel good about yourself!

Step 5: Evaluate

The final step of the decluttering method is to evaluate, which is the step that is the most easily skipped. Change is a cyclical process. We go through small cycles, one at a time, to reach a bigger transformation goal. As I suggested earlier, you might find that this goal shifts a bit as you go. You might find that as you peel back the emotional layers, you are not in fact dealing with what you thought you were, and your emotional discovery journey might lead you somewhere different than you were expecting.

So this step is an important one for the process. You want to be able to reflect after each small action and check that you are still following the same initial goal or if you need to reframe your work. You might also discover new emotions appearing in your landscape that were either not there before, you didn't notice, or were buried a bit deeper and now have the space to surface. So you go through the cycle again with your new information. Alternatively, you might find a huge resistance both in yourself or in others to a new version of you. How attached are you or others to your current emotional state? What threat would you or they face if your emotional state evolved? There are no quick fixes, but everything is possible. Here are some reflection questions to help you with this step.

1. How did the fear of facing your emotions compare with the discomfort of actually doing it?
2. What is becoming easier for you as a result of engaging with and facing your emotions?
3. What are you learning about yourself through your emotions? Are you noticing them morphing as you bring them to light?
4. Consider what enabled you to achieve this. What can you tap into next time you are facing a similar situation?

5. Expanding the learning, how could you use this insight or behavior and replicate the success in other areas?

This concludes Part 3 about your emotional clutter and closes the circle on the three-part model. This area is perhaps the trickiest to work on, and I am beginning to regard it as a lifelong exercise in self-discovery and awareness of everything that I have accumulated and am unknowingly carrying with me.

Suppressing and hiding away your emotions will not serve you in the long run. Emotions that we deny will trouble us, interfere with our thinking, steal our attention in ways we can't put our finger on, but they will clutter us. The only way forward is to acknowledge these emotions and bring them out into the light so that they become our guide, helping us see more clearly and devise a path forward that will be true to what we desire.

I don't suggest for one second that this will be easy, but if you want to live a lighter life and feel agency in what you are doing, then you need to acknowledge and accept what is inside you. Learning to listen to your feelings and emotions will liberate you from the grasp they have on you, and then you can move forward. Or simply stay right where you are if you so wish but live with greater ease. That's fine too, as long as it's your choice.

Chapter summary

- Emotions are part and parcel of being human and acknowledging them will give you greater insight into who you are.
- Step 1: Surveying your emotions can be a scary prospect, but the fear of looking is likely to be worse than the reality of facing them.
- Step 2: Plan what you would like your emotional landscape to look like and what you want to be feeling.
- Step 3: Act on your plan by starting with the small and simple tasks when the time is right. Shifting your familiar emotional responses to situations might encounter some resistance!
- Step 4: Celebrate every little gain you make, every small shift toward your new desired emotional state.
- Step 5: Evaluate your learnings through the reflection questions and by noticing every new emotional response to what you are experimenting with.

13

Beyond this book: uncluttered for life

This book has covered a lot of ground and touched on many different topics and areas, not all of which will be relevant for you right now. My hope is that you will take away what is useful, and store away the rest for future reference when it becomes timely and you encounter different situations.

I strongly believe, from my personal experience and from working with clients over the years, that decluttering is not only a way to live more lightly and freely but is also essential if you want to start something new. People often begin a major decluttering exercise when they are going through a big life change such as a new job, a separation or a house move. The desire to shed some of the old when stepping into a new phase of life is not uncommon, perhaps becoming a slightly different version of ourselves as we grow with new experiences.

Even if you are not embarking on anything new in your life, paying attention to the clutter in your landscape will bring benefits that you can't always predict. When Jenny started her project of decluttering the stacks and stacks of paper she had accumulated over many years of running a design business, her goal was to create physical space to use her office as an art studio. What she came away with was a greater understanding of the speed her mind was running at and how it regularly tripped her up. She gained a sense of focus and clarity of thought that brought her calmness, and that was as transformational as the ability to use her office space differently. It offered her insights into what she could experiment with in other areas of her life, too, such as how she could simply be and listen more intently to her elderly parents rather than rush to do things for them, or how she could set some boundaries and protect her time when necessary.

Developing a decluttering mindset

Participants in my decluttering program often join the course with one specific goal and then find that over the following months or years, other chapters and sections resonate with them and they return to the material to revisit different areas of the program. As events and situations arise in their lives, they adapt and handle them as best they can. As you continue to collect experiences that shape you and your worldview, as you evolve over time, you might want to consider how you can make your efforts sustainable. A point that often comes up when I talk about a decluttering process is how to move from a big, one-off exercise of clearing all the desired areas to developing an ongoing decluttering mindset. Here are some thoughts to prompt your thinking:

- For a start, going through a decluttering effort will naturally make you look at your clutter differently. It's similar to being on a diet, where you pay attention to and notice your food or drink intake, which you perhaps didn't before. Similarly, the act of tidying up and engaging with your clutter will make you pay attention and notice the stuff around you far more. And in the same way, it will help you notice it when an excess of stuff starts to reappear.

- Remind yourself of your purpose for wanting to create space in the first place – be it physical, mental or emotional space. You had deep and meaningful reasons for wanting to do this, so refer back to these regularly until they are so familiar that they are a part of you. You might also find a visual representation of your purpose; many people find pictures or other visual prompts to be a useful guide.

- When considering physical clutter, remember the 'time to tidy' that you are comfortable with. It gives you a framework, a measure that you can gauge your clutter level against. Again, visual reminders of these in each area might be helpful.

- Noticing your habits around the acquisition of clutter is also an important part of the process. Often, patterns developed over a long period of time might originate from somewhere that is not immediately obvious.

- The world, your job and your life will throw endless

mental clutter at you. Unless you protect your valuable brain processing power, you will continue to feel at the mercy of external forces. Making technology work for you by disabling all its built-in distractions and actively filtering out of your mental landscape what you don't need right now will reduce the deluge of data coming in. Creating new habits around journaling, mindfulness or other techniques will help to clear your mind.

- Bringing to light and accepting your emotional clutter is what will be the most transformational of all. I have seen this again and again when running my program: attendees join because they have physical clutter to work through, and after some time realize that the barriers are all related to their emotions in one way or another. Slowly releasing the fear of embracing these emotions is what allows true personal growth, and it is also the most rewarding!

Shifting your habits around consumption

Excessive clutter can come at a heavy cost, and I have often heard people describe how having all this stuff literally feels like an oppressive weight on their shoulders. Buying fewer items, of better quality and more locally, can have a huge impact not only on our purses but also on our wellbeing, our community and the planet (Grant 2024).

I want to share this final client story with you as it is such a good illustration of the complexities of ownership and clutter, how its patterns around accumulation aren't always obvious, and how significant a change of behavior can be.

Tim had come to me for some coaching around navigating a challenging situation at work. He was finding it difficult to engage with some of his colleagues, whom he didn't trust, and he felt that his voice was not being heard at the table. In our work together, he identified that what he felt was deep anger and hurt at his manager and colleagues because some work that he had done was not being recognized, and he was not given the due credit for it.

Tim then realized that over many years, he had developed a habit of purchasing luxury items that he could not afford whenever he felt angry or hurt, creating significant financial pressure and causing himself and his family a lot of stress. Realizing what he was doing and acknowledging his patterns allowed Tim to adjust his course.

He recognized that his current way of handling things wasn't making him happy. He identified new habits that he wanted to switch to when he felt the urge of the buying impulse and decided to openly address his feelings with his manager and colleagues in an adult manner by stepping out of the drama triangle and into a choiceful, mature place. His new habits had a huge impact not only on his bank balance but also on his overall mood and the relationship with his family and his colleagues.

Understanding what your habits are around gathering clutter will help you become better equipped to identify your desired new behaviors and shift toward them. It is difficult to *stop* doing something. However, *choosing to do something different* in a specific circumstance or on the back of a trigger is far easier and can have considerable results. For example, rather than focusing on trying to stop a habit of doomscrolling on your newsfeed first thing in the morning, divert this habit instead to starting a new one of looking out of the window with a cup of tea/coffee/other beverage of choice and thinking about the one thing you want to get done today.

Understanding how your stuff got there in the first place is the starting point for creating a different set of habits. Be it physical, mental or emotional stuff, understanding what is typical for you is what then allows you to identify what might need to change to create a simpler, lighter and calmer life. I wish you well on your own decluttering path, and if you have any clutter stories that you would like to share, please do send them to me. I would love to read them.

To finish, don't let this book become clutter for you. Think about who would benefit from it and pass it on!

In spaciousness,
Ingrid
startcreatingspace.com

Acknowledgments

Thank you to the whole team at The Right Book Company for helping me create a book from my ideas! It was quite the project but made so much more manageable with your guidance.

Thank you to all my clients who have trusted me with their stories, taught me so much about how clutter affects them in a myriad of ways and inspired me to develop this work. You have remained anonymous throughout this book but not in my mind.

Thank you to my coaching supervisor Andrew Machon, who was the first person to see my passion in this field all those years ago and encouraged me to have confidence in my inspiration. I wouldn't have gone down this path without that early nudge. And what an honor to receive your foreword.

A heartfelt thank you to Stephen Karpman for the permission to reproduce the drama triangle, and for the further insights into how clutter can play out in various ways, openly and covertly, in relationships with others and oneself.

Huge gratitude to my dear colleagues and friends, Barry Joinson and Joanna Young, who supported me along the way and continue to unfailingly root for me. I could not keep doing this without you!

Thank you to my brother Albert Cohen, my tech support, who is always on hand to answer all my questions and makes navigating the digital space easy. That is an extraordinary gift in this world.

And finally, Nick, for the illustrations, for the cheerleading, for everything. You make this possible.

Appendix 1

The language of emotions

I have presented these words in columns representing intensity (see next page). This can help you not only be more precise when you describe an emotion but also open up the possibility that there can be different intensities at which you experience situations. For example, you might feel anger in all these situations, but the intensity of each might be different:

- angry with the supermarket staff because the self-service checkout machine got stuck again
- angry with your partner because they forgot to book those tickets you wanted
- angry with your boss because they did not support you in a meeting
- angry with your child because they disobeyed you
- etc...

This resource is available to download from my website at startcreatingspace.com/book

Anger

soft	medium	intense
annoyed	affronted	contemptuous
critical	aggravated	enraged
cynical	bristling	furious
envious	defiant	irate
frustrated	exasperated	livid
grumpy	indignant	seething
impatient	offended	spiteful
irritated	resentful	vindictive

Disgust

soft	medium	intense
apathetic	critical	disgusted
averse	disappointed	disliking
bored	disapproving	hating
hesitant	judgmental	loathing
indifferent	rejected	repulsed
uninterested	unfriendly	revolted

Fear

soft	medium	intense
apprehensive	alarmed	appalled
cautious	distrustful	desperate
concerned	guarded	dreading
disconcerted	perturbed	frantic
edgy	rattled	horrified
insecure	shaken	panicked
tentative	suspicious	paralyzed
unsure	unnerved	petrified
worried	unsettled	shocked

Joy

soft	medium	intense
amused	assured	awe-filled
content	cheerful	blissful
flattered	confident	elated
fortunate	contented	exhilarated
glad	delighted	fulfilled
hopeful	joyful	jubilant
inspired	optimistic	overjoyed
peaceful	pleased	proud
pleased	upbeat	thrilled
serene	valued	uplifted

Sadness

soft	medium	intense
brooding	dejected	anguished
distracted	dispirited	bereaved
listless	grieving	depressed
low	heavy-hearted	despairing
pensive	melancholy	despondent
regretful	mournful	grief-stricken
sad	sorrowful	heartbroken
wistful	weepy	inconsolable

Surprise

soft	medium	intense
ambivalent	discombobulated	astonished
directionless	flustered	amazed
distracted	impressed	baffled
uncertain	perplexed	bewildered
uncomfortable	puzzled	constricted
unsettled	shocked	stunned
unsure	startled	trapped

Appendix 2

Subpersonality exercise

This exercise is designed to document your thoughts and reflections when you encounter one of your subpersonalities. These will often be more noticeable when you find yourself on the negative side of the emotional scale and feeling dissatisfied, upset, fearful, hurt or disappointed. Spend time getting to know the part of you that is showing up in that moment and feeling these feelings by going through the following steps:

1. Give that part of you a name. This can be anything you like!
2. Ask yourself what that part of you is experiencing and feeling. Tap into all your new knowledge about emotions to be as specific as possible.
3. What does that part of you want?
4. What does that part of you need?
5. How is that part of you keeping you safe?
6. How could that part help you grow?

The purpose of this exercise is to get to know yourself better, so you want to do this with kindness for yourself. Judgment is never useful, and it certainly has no place in this exercise.

Example:

Name:	Scaredycat
What is this part of me feeling?	Scaredycat feels scared and fearful, doesn't like taking risks and is worried that others will make fun and take advantage.
What does this part of me want?	Scaredycat wants me to stay right where I am, wants to feel safe and not be put into uncomfortable situations.
What does this part of me need?	Scaredycat needs reassurance and needs to feel in control, needs to stay with what's familiar.
How is this part of me keeping me safe?	Scaredycat is looking out for me and protecting me from making poor decisions, bad choices, or the judgment of others.
How could this part of me help me grow?	Scaredycat can be a useful radar to keep me from jumping into situations unprepared. It can help me identify that I need to carry out my research before I commit.

This resource is available to download from my website at start-creatingspace.com/book.

References

Appleton, J (2018) 'The Gut–Brain Axis: Influence of
microbiota on mood and mental health'. *Integrative
Medicine* 17(4).

Arnsten, A (2009) 'Stress signalling pathways that impair
prefrontal cortex structure and function'. *Nature Reviews
Neuroscience* 10(6).

Assagioli, R (2000) *Psychosynthesis: A manual of principles and
techniques.* Thorsons.

AXA (2023) 'The true cost of running on empty:
Work-related stress costing UK economy £28bn a year'.
AXA Newsroom 29 March. URL: axa.co.uk/newsroom/
media-releases/2023/the-true-cost-of-running-on-empty-
work-related-stress-costing-uk-economy-28bn-a-year

Baikie, K A & Wilhelm, K (2005) 'Emotional and physical
health benefits of expressive writing'. *Advances in
Psychiatric Treatment* 11(5).

Becker, M W & Leinenger, M (2011) 'Attentional selection is
biased toward mood-congruent stimuli'. *Emotion* 11(5).

Berboth, S & Morawetz, C (2021) 'Amygdala-prefrontal
connectivity during emotion regulation: A meta-analysis
of psychophysiological interactions'. *Neuropsychologia* 153.

Berry, W (1970) *Farming: A hand book.* Harcourt.

Bhave, V M, Oladele, C R et al (2024) 'Associations between
ultra-processed food consumption and adverse brain
health outcomes'. *Neurology* 102(11).

Boniwell, I & Tunariu, A D (2019) *Positive Psychology: Theory, research and applications.* McGraw Hill.

Brackett, M (2019) *Permission to Feel: Unlocking the power of emotions to help our kids, ourselves, and our society thrive.* Celadon Books.

Brown, B (2021) *Atlas of the Heart: Mapping meaningful connection and the language of human experience.* Random House.

Cartwright, R D (2012) *The Twenty-four Hour Mind: The role of sleep and dreaming in our emotional lives.* Oxford University Press.

Chamine, S (2012) *Positive Intelligence: Why only 20% of teams and individuals achieve their true potential and how you can achieve yours.* Greenleaf Book Group LLC.

Choy, A (1990) 'The Winner's Triangle'. *Transactional Analysis Journal* 20(1).

Clear, J (2018) *Atomic Habits: An easy & proven way to build good habits & break bad ones.* Random House Business.

Cohen, M A, Cavanagh, P et al (2012) 'The attentional requirements of consciousness'. *Trends in Cognitive Sciences* 16(8).

Collins English Dictionary (2025) HarperCollins Publishers.

Diehl, M, Hay, E L & Berg, K M (2011) 'The ratio between positive and negative affect and flourishing mental health across adulthood'. *Aging & Mental Health* 15(7).

Ekstedt, N & Ennart, H (2018) *Happy Food: How eating well can lift your mood and bring you joy.* Bloomsbury Publishing.

Esposito, F & Ferreira, T M C (2024) 'Addictive design as an unfair commercial practice: The case of hyper-engaging dark patterns'. *European Journal of Risk Regulation* 15(4).

Eugene, A R & Masiak, J (2015) 'The neuroprotective aspects of sleep'. *MEDtube Sci.* 3(1).

Eyal, N (2019) *Indistractable: How to control your attention and choose your life*. Bloomsbury Publishing PLC.

Feldman Barrett (2017) 'Many fairy tales about the brain still propagate through our field'. *The British Psychological Society*, 31 January. URL: bps.org.uk/psychologist/many-fairy-tales-about-brain-still-propagate-through-our-field

Feldman Barrett, L (2018) 'The three big myths about emotions, gender and brains'. *Wired UK,* 9 January. URL: youtu.be/9WFPBey02b0

Feldman Barrett, L (2021) *Seven and a Half Lessons About the Brain*. Picador.

Ford, B Q, Lam, P et al (2018) 'The psychological health benefits of accepting negative emotions and thoughts: Laboratory, diary, and longitudinal evidence'. *Journal of Personality and Social Psychology* 115(6).

Fosslien, L & West Duffy, M (2019) *No Hard Feelings: The secret power of embracing emotions at work*. Portfolio Penguin.

Fredrickson, B L (2004) 'The broaden-and-build theory of positive emotions'. *Philosophical Transactions of the Royal Society London B* 359(1449).

Fredrickson, B L (2009) *Positivity: Groundbreaking research reveals how to embrace the hidden strength of positive emotions, overcome negativity, and thrive*. Crown Archetype.

Gomes Gonçalves, N, Vidal Ferreira, N et al (2023) 'Association between consumption of ultraprocessed foods and cognitive decline'. *JAMA Neurology* 80(2).

Grant, P (2024) *Less: Stop buying so much rubbish: How having fewer, better things can make us happier*. HarperCollins Publishers.

Grossman, P, Niemann, L et al (2004) 'Mindfulness-based stress reduction and health benefits: A meta-analysis'.

Journal of Psychosomatic Research 57(1).

Hall, S S (2013) 'Repairing bad memories'. *MIT Technology Review* 17 June. URL: technologyreview.com/2013/06/17/177763/repairing-bad-memories

Harvard Medical School (2020) 'Exercising to relax: How does exercise reduce stress? Surprising answers to this question and more.' *Harvard Health Publishing,* 7 July. URL: health.harvard.edu/staying-healthy/exercising-to-relax

Hood, B (2020) *Possessed: Why we want more than we need.* Penguin.

Kahneman, D (2012) *Thinking, Fast and Slow.* Penguin.

Karpman, S B (1968) 'Fairy tales and script drama analysis'. *Transactional Analysis Bulletin* 7(26). URL: https://karpmandramatriangle.com/pdf/DramaTriangle.pdf.

Karpman, S B (2014) *A Game Free Life.* Drama Triangle Publications.

Killgore, W D S (2010) 'Effects of sleep deprivation on cognition'. *Progress in Brain Research* Vol 185.

Knezevic, E, Nenic, K et al (2023) 'The role of cortisol in chronic stress, neurodegenerative diseases, and psychological disorders'. *Cells* 12(23).

Kondo, M (2014) *The Life-Changing Magic of Tidying: A simple, effective way to banish clutter forever.* Ebury Publishing.

Levitin, D (2014) *The Organized Mind: The science of preventing overload, increasing productivity and restoring your focus.* Penguin.

Levitin, D (2015) 'Why the modern world is bad for your brain'. *The Guardian* 18 Jan URL: theguardian.com/science/2015/jan/18/modern-world-bad-for-brain-daniel-j-levitin-organized-mind-information-overload

Lieberman, M D & Torre, J B (2018) 'Putting feelings into words: Affect labeling as implicit emotion regulation'. *Emotion Review* 10(2).

Mojtahedi, D (2017) 'New research reveals how little we can trust eyewitnesses'. *The Conversation,* 13 July. URL: theconversation.com/new-research-reveals-how-little-we-can-trust-eyewitnesses-67663

Morris, W (1882) *Hopes and Fears for Art: Five lectures delivered in Birmingham, London, and Nottingham 1878-1881.* Ellis & White.

Mujica, A L, Crowell, C R et al (2022) 'Addiction by design: Some dimensions and challenges of excessive social media use'. *Medical Research Archives* 10(2).

Nekoei, A, Sigurdsson J & Wehr, D (2024) 'The economics of burnout'. *VOXEU Column,* 22 June. URL: cepr.org/voxeu/columns/economics-burnout

Newport, C (2024) *Slow Productivity: The lost art of accomplishment without burnout.* Penguin Business.

NHS (2022) 'Stress'. URL: nhs.uk/mental-health/feelings-symptoms-behaviours/feelings-and-symptoms/stress/

NHS (2023) 'Coping with financial worries'. URL: nhs.uk/mental-health/advice-for-life-situations-and-events/how-to-cope-with-financial-worries/

Nummenmaa, L, Glerean, E et al (2014) 'Bodily maps of emotions'. *Proceedings of the National Academy of Sciences U.S.A.* 111 (2).

Oatley, K, Keltner, D & Jenkins, J M (2006) *Understanding Emotions.* Blackwell Publishing.

Oxford Languages Dictionary (2025) Oxford University Press.

Pennebaker, J W (1997) *Opening up: The healing power of expressing emotions.* The Guildford Press.

Peters, S (2012) *The Chimp Paradox: The mind management*

programme to help you achieve success, confidence and happiness. Vermilion.

Pink, D (2018) *When: The scientific secrets of perfect timing.* Canongate Books.

Pitts, M A, Lutsyshyna, L A & Hillyard, S A (2018) 'The relationship between attention and consciousness: An expanded taxonomy and implications for "no-report" paradigms'. *Royal Society* 373(1755).

Raphael, R (2017) 'Netflix CEO Reed Hastings: Sleep is our competition'. *Fast Company,* 11 June. URL: fastcompany.com/40491939/netflix-ceo-reed-hastings-sleep-is-our-competition

Raskin, A (2019) 'One of my lessons from infinite scroll: That optimizing something for ease-of-use does not mean best for the user or humanity'. X, 11 June. URL: x.com/aza/status/1138268959982022656

Raypole, C (2022) 'How to do a body scan meditation (and why you should)'. *Healthline* 5 December. URL: healthline.com/health/body-scan-meditation

Roster, C A, Ferrari, J R & Jurkat, M P (2016) 'The dark side of home: Assessing possession "clutter" on subjective well-being'. *Journal of Environmental Psychology* 46.

Russell, J A (1980) 'Circumplex model of affect'. *Journal of Personality and Social Psychology* 39(6).

Sacks, O (2017) *The River of Consciousness.* Picador.

Salovey, P & Mayer, J D (1990) 'Emotional Intelligence'. *Imagination, Cognition and Personality* 9(3).

Saxbe, D & Repetti, R (2010) 'No place like home: Home tours correlate with daily patterns of mood and cortisol'. *Personality and Social Psychology Bulletin* 36(1).

Schiller, D, Monfils, M H et al (2010) 'Preventing the return of fear in humans using reconsolidation update mechanisms'. *Nature* 463 (7277).

Shapiro, J (2021) 'Two parts of the brain govern much of mental life: Understanding the roles of the amygdala and the prefrontal cortex'. *Psychology Today,* 5 November. URL: psychologytoday.com/intl/blog/thinking-in-black-white-and-gray/202111/two-parts-the-brain-govern-much-mental-life

Shirky, C (2008) 'Web 2.0 Expo NY: It's not information overload. It's filter failure'. URL: youtu.be/LabqeJEOQyI

Song, Z, Song, R et al (2023) 'Effects of ultra-processed foods on the microbiota-gut-brain axis: The bread-and-butter issue'. *Food Research International* 167(112730).

Statista (2024) 'Volume of data/information created, captured, copied, and consumed worldwide from 2010 to 2023, with forecasts from 2024 to 2028'. URL: statista.com/statistics/871513/worldwide-data-created

Stewart, W (2010) 'Highrise horror'. *Firefighting in Canada,* 25 November. URL: firefightingincanada.com/highrise-horror-7328

Vaillant, J (2023) *Fire Weather: A true story from a hotter world.* Sceptre.

Veepara, E, Grandgenevre, P et al (2020) 'Attentional bias towards negative stimuli in healthy individuals and the effects of trait anxiety'. *Scientific Reports* 10(11826).

Walker, M (2018) *Why We Sleep: The new science of sleep and dreams.* Penguin.

Williams, J (2020) 'Is our attention for sale?' *RSA Short,* 27 August. URL: youtu.be/PSaybP1UivQ

Wright, P (2023) 'Men tend to regulate their emotions through actions rather than words'. *Male Psychology: The Magazine,* 1 August. URL: centreformalepsychology.com/male-psychology-magazine-listings/men-tend-to-regulate-their-emotions-through-actions-rather-than-words

Wu, T (2017) 'The crisis of attention theft – ads that steal your time for nothing in return'. *Wired,* 14 April. URL: wired.com/2017/04/forcing-ads-captive-audience-attention-theft-crime

About the author

Ingrid Pope is an executive coach and expert declutterer. Having previously worked in corporate IT, she combined a lifelong interest in organizing spaces with her professional experience to set up her business, Creating Space. Through her work, Ingrid aims to raise awareness of how reducing the clutter, the busyness, and the noise are essential for maximizing our effectiveness and reclaiming our agency.

She has also been involved with the Future of Coaching Collaboration since 2019, facilitating conversations around how technology is changing the coaching industry.

Outside of working and writing, Ingrid enjoys reading and getting involved in her local community in Tunbridge Wells, Kent.

EU Safety Representative: euComply OÜ Pärnu mnt 139b-14 11317 Tallinn
Estonia hello@eucompliancepartner.com +33 756 90241

www.ingramcontent.com/pod-product-compliance
Lightning Source LLC
Chambersburg PA
CBHW021142090426
42740CB00008B/900